THE S
OF TRUTH

Edited by

TONY ORTZEN

The Spiritual Truth Press

First published in 1987
Rreprinted 1998

The Spiritual Truth Press
15 Broom Hall, Oxshott
Surrey KT22 0JZ

ISBN 0 85384 105 5

Printed in Great Britain by Booksprint

Foreword

There are a number of possible reasons why you are reading this book. The first and most likely is that you are already a 'follower' of Silver Birch and have found his great wisdom and spiritual insights of benefit in your life. In this case you will welcome this reprint of one of the classic books of his teachings. Maybe you have been given this book by a friend who believes its message of love, in this world and the next, will inspire or comfort you. If so, you will not be dissappointed.

Perhaps you chanced upon it on a bookshelf or saw it advertised, then curiosity got the better of you. Well, after reading its pages you may also decide that 'chance' played no part in the decision and that some form of spiritual guidance has brought you and this book together.

Whatever the reason, the chances are that Silver Birchs's wisdom will remain with you forever. Long after you have forgotten his precise words, his guidance will still be a very real influence whenever you need it. And if you need to jog your memory - just reach for this book and read it again. Silver Birch's words are so accessible and meaningful that you will never tire of reading them. But who is Siver Birch, the spirit guide whose words are faithfully recorded here? And who was Maurice Barbanell, the London medium who channelled that wisdom? Without an answer to these qestions, many new readers - however impressed with these teachings - will be puzzled about their source.

Barbanell was the founder and editor of a weekly Spiritualist newspaper, *Psychic News*, and for half a century devoted his life to spreading spiritual knowledge through its columns and those of other publications with which he was associated. In his own obituary, which he wrote before his passing at the age of 79 on July 17th 1981, he revealed that he was told by Estelle Roberts' Red Cloud - a spirit guide for whom he had the greatest admiration - that in a previous incarnation he had made a promise to reincarnate and devote his life to spreading Spiritualism. Though he had no knowledge of that life or promise, events certainly conspired to make it possible.

He was born to Jewish parents in a poor area of London's East End. His mother was devoutly religious but his father, a barber, was an atheist so Barbanell heard many arguments about religion during his early years. His father always won, and his son adopted the same outlook but later changed to agnosticism. Yet after hearing about Spiritualism from a speaker at a social and literary club of which he was secretary, Barbanell refused to start the debate by putting an opposing view - one of his duties - because, he explained, he had made no personal investigation and therefore his opinions were valueless. This impressed the speaker who invited Barbanell to attend a sceance in which a medium, Mrs Blaustein, was entranced by various spirits of different nationalities. He was not impressed, and on a second visit fell asleep. Barbanell apologised, believing that either boredom or tiredness had been responsible, but the other circle members informed him that he had not been asleep but had been in trance and a Red Indian had spoken through him.

With the enccouragement of famous Fleet Street journalist Hannen Swaffer, Barbanell founded *Psychic News* partly as a vehicle for the guide's teachings. But, because he knew he would be criticised for publishing his own mediumship in his own newspaper, Barbanell did not reveal to his readers for many years who was channelling the wisdom, by which time the guide had a huge following on his own merits.

Silver Birch spoke regularly at Barbanell's home circle and the proceedings were always recorded in shorthand. There were a number of diffferences in style and procedure between Barbanell's own journalistic efforts and the way in which Silver Birch communicated, as Barbanell himself observed:

"In my working life I use words every day. I have never yet written or dictated an article with which I was satisfied when I read it. Inevitably I find, when looking at the typed material, that I can improve it by altering words, phrases and sentences. No such problem arises with the guide's teachings. These flow perfectly, requiring usually only punctuation. Another interesting aspect is the occasional use of words that I regard as archaic and do not form part of my normal vocabulary."

But who was Silver Birch? A psychic artist depicts him as a serious-looking native American Indian with a single feather and compassionate eyes. There is evidence to suggest that this was simply a convenient *persona* behind which a far more spiritually-evolved soul hid in order that those who read his words would judge them not by the name attached to them but by the wisdom that pervades every sentence.

Those of us who knew them both were well aware of the differences in the way they spoke and the words they used. They both had spiritual missions and they fulfilled them admirably, particularly when working together in their unique two-world partnership. This, as you are about to discover, has provided us with simple, uplifting, comforting and inspirational answers to the questions we all ask, from time to time, about life and its purpose. They are needed now more than ever before as we prepare for the challenges that will confront us in the 21st century.

Roy Stemman
Chairman
Spiritual Truth Foundation

The Silver Birch Books

Teachings of Silver Birch	first published in 1938
Guidance from Silver Birch	first published in 1966
Philosophy of Silver Birch	first published in 1969
More Philosophy of Siver Birch	first published in 1979
Light from Silver Birch	first published in 1983
Silver Birch Companion	first published in 1986
A Voice in the Wilderness	first published in 1986
The Seed of Truth	first published in 1987
The Spirit Speaks	first published in 1988
Lift Up Your Hearts	first published in 1990
The Universe of Silver Birch	first published in 1994
The Silver Birch Book of Questions and Answers	first published in 1998

The Cassette, "Silver Birch Speaks", recorded at the Hannen Swaffer Home Circle, is available from Psychic Press.

The Spiritual Truth Press is the publishing arm of **The Spiritual Truth Foundation** which is a charity established to assist needy Spiritualists and Medium as well as to help to spread spiritual truths by financing the publication of new and classic books on subjects relevant to our understanding of man's nature and destiny.

All proceeds from the sale of this book will go to the Foundation to further its work. To that end it welcomes donations and bequests.

For further information about The Spiritual Truth Foundation contact the Secretary at 15 Broom Hall, Oxshott, Surrey KT22 0JZ

CONTENTS

DEDICATION

"THE seed of truth cannot grow where the heart is hard and the mind is stony, but can flourish only where there is a receptive soul, one who is ready to receive truth and to follow truth wherever she leads.

"Before you can be so inclined, before you are ready for truth to dwell in your midst, you must have endured some of those experiences which life provides in order to make you ready for truth.

"When you had those experiences you may have thought that life was bitter and harsh and unkind, that you were forgotten, or lonely, or neglected, and fate had dealt you a very hard blow. But the soul grows through adversity and the pure gold emerges after the processes of crushing and refining have taken place.

"If you are about to read the words that follow, then you can say, with all sincerity, you are ready for truth. That does not mean you are called upon to accept all that is written here if the words strike disagreement in your mind. Reject everything that is contrary to your reason; discard everything that is foreign to your common sense.

"I am only a human being just as you are, but I have trod a few more steps along the roadway of life and I have retraced those steps to tell you what lies ahead of you when you cross the threshold of death to enter the new and wider life that is your inevitable destiny.

"So approach truth with humility and with reverence, for with these qualities she will be a welcome guest in your life. Encourage her to stay, for she brings with her assurance, certainty, understanding and, above all, the priceless gift of knowledge which endures for all time."—Silver Birch.

INTRODUCTION

IF you stopped an average member of the public in the street and asked if they believed that a long-dead Red Indian could return and speak on all manner of subjects, they would probably beat a hasty retreat!

But how wrong and misled are those who assume or assert that physical death is the end, that as the last breath is drawn, life is snuffed out like a candle being extinguished. For as Spiritualists know, one's time on earth is but a tiny proportion of human existence.

We believe—and have evidence to back our claim—that life in the spirit world is a reality and that the so-called dead can and do return, as has been proven thousands of times throughout history.

Silver Birch's earthly mission ended one July night in 1981 when his medium, Maurice Barbanell, passed on. How glad both must now be from the spiritual realms that his words are still being read, appreciated and disseminated throughout the world.

Silver Birch is a master of oratory. Sadly, these days, our world seems to become ever increasingly violent. It is against this backdrop that his words and philosophy are truly an oasis in a material maelstrom.

More than that, the ever-patient guide proves that the dead can communicate; that they retain their characteristics and memories; that they are reasoning, intelligent beings; that they care about those left behind; that once freed from physical limitations they have a wider perspective.

"The Seed of Truth" is based upon two much earlier Silver Birch volumes, "Silver Birch Speaks" and "More Wisdom of Silver Birch." They were published in 1949 and 1945. Both were compiled by Sylvia Barbanell, the medium's wife, who weekly—and later monthly—sat next to her husband as he slipped into trance and temporarily opened the veil between two worlds.

The questions asked and admirably answered in this book are as varied as those that put them. Would Silver Birch comment on cremation? What were his views on psychical research? How do the dead pass their time? Are there houses, books and food in the afterlife? Is suffering necessary to develop one's character? Do the Ten Commandments need to be rewritten? Should patients receive treatment from more than one spiritual healer?

All these points—and many, many more—were put to the guide. And never once did Silver Birch refuse to answer a question; never once did he stumble or find himself lost for an answer. For no matter how abstruse the question put to the guide, his reply came cogently, convincingly and instantly.

As a journalist, I am used to editing articles and features. It never ceases to amaze me that Silver Birch's words rarely need alteration or rephrasing. His mastery of the English language is unparalleled.

In my office hangs a beautiful colour portrait of Silver Birch, painted by the psychic artist Marcel Poncin. It was a Christmas present in 1937 to the Barbanells from Hannen Swaffer and his wife, spirit healers Billy and Peggy Parish and journalist Paul Harris and his wife Fay.

For over 40 years the picture rightly had pride of place in the Barbanells' St. John's Wood, NW London, flat. Now it hangs in the editorial offices of "Psychic News," a fitting tribute to both medium and guide, since Maurice Barbanell founded the paper.

Though the wise words in this book were delivered by Silver Birch some years ago, they have lost none of their timeless wisdom. They are applicable to all, be they commoner or king.

I hope that all who read this volume will find renewed strength, vigour and determination, that within these pages the troubled may find peace of mind and hope for the future.

TONY ORTZEN.

Chapter One

'THE ILLUSION OF TIME'

"HOW do the dead pass their time?" Silver Birch was asked at one circle gathering. "Have they time just as we have with hours of light and darkness, or is it another sort of time? What do they do? Do they work or study, or amuse themselves?"

The guide replied: "That has been answered many, many times. The question of time is one of interest because we are not dependent on your definition of time.

"Yours is a demarcation for purposes of convenience. That is, you have charted certain passages as minutes or hours, or seconds, or days, and all that is based upon the rotation of the earth and its relationship to the sun. We do not have night and day. Our source of light is not the same as yours. Therefore, we do not have time in the sense in which you have it. Our measurement of time depends upon our spiritual state, that is, we feel time in the sense of enjoyment. Time, to us, is a mental experience.

"In the lower spheres, where life is not very enjoyable, it seems a long time to them. In higher spheres—and I am speaking relatively—where there is much more congenial activity, time seems more speedy in the sense that there is always some new phase of interesting labour. But it is not apportioned in hours, or days, or months, or years. As to the way in which we work, that depends on the individual. There is plenty of activity connected with the mind and the spirit.

"The difficulty the questioner has is in understanding spiritual experiences in terms of physical measurement, but there are wide and boundless pursuits of the mind and the spirit, cultural, educational, purposive, actual in their effect on your physical world, to engage us and occupy us for as long as we wish to be so occupied."

"But," asked a sitter, "the question arises—if you want to book something ahead, how do you do it, if time has no meaning as it has here?"

"Do you mean," asked the guide, "if I wished to meet someone? Then I send a thought and if it is convenient we meet. There are no letters to be written."

"What if you wanted to arrange to meet somebody at some specified time?"

"It does not happen that way," was the answer. "The only kind of engagement like that is the perpetuation of the earthly custom of festivals, such as my retirement at what approximates to your Easter and your Christmas. That is a withdrawal from your world, but that is only a convenience. I could, if it were necessary, retire to those spheres when I have finished speaking with this instrument. If I am desired to attend some group, the request is sent to me mentally, I receive it and I go. It would not be sent to me now because it would be known that I am at this moment speaking with you. There are no diaries; it is a world of the mind and of the spirit."

Someone in the circle asked if there were trains in the spirit world, and the guide answered: "There are no trains unless you think you have a train to catch and then there is a train for you to catch. It is hard to understand, isn't it? But it is like a dream. If you think you have a train to catch, there is your train.

"Even in your dreams you think you have to go on a ship. The ship is there because you make the ship, and it is real to you. You people it and it travels. It has got the necessary attendants, hasn't it? It is very real on its own plane of sensation. You must remember that reality is a relative term."

"I have heard and read of these things frequently," said a

sitter, "but I must say it is very difficult for me to appreciate."

"It is," said Silver Birch. "But even in your world you have the illusion of time. One hour is not always the same to you; and five minutes can sometimes seem as long as one hour. That is the mental aspect of it. If you appreciate that in our world that mental aspect is the reality, you will see that we are divorced from the purely mechanical aspect of time as it affects you. I think that is the best way to express it."

Another question sent in was, "Does each individual have a house of his own?"

"Yes," replied the guide, "they have houses of their own if they want them, because they desire them and they earn them. But some do not desire houses. Some prefer them built according to their own styles of architecture, some prefer to incorporate ideas of lighting which are, for example, not known to you. This is a matter of personal taste dependent upon the creative ability of the spirit concerned."

"Didn't you say," a member of the circle interposed, "that your house was dependent upon the kind of life you had lived?"

"I said," went on Silver Birch, "if you desired it and had earned it. But once you have earned it, then its style is purely a matter of taste. If you would like it open to the sky you can have it. You must remember that these things are largely controlled for a long time by individual habit. Habit is a mental attribute and it persists after death.

"People who have dwelt only in this country are accustomed to certain styles of houses and thus it is those styles in which they live because it is a habit to do so. Once they have outworn that habit they have other types of houses. This is a very wise provision which ensures continuity; it prevents shock and life is smoother and more harmonious as a result."

With these words the guide ended the sitting: "I have come back very close to you all. I would like you to know that I am closer to each one of you than ever I have been before and this will provide me with the opportunity of giving, I hope, even greater service to those who are closest to me in the bond of that love which binds us all together in unity of purpose.

"And let us always remember the great central purpose which unites us. Let us remember that always our task is directed to the less fortunate ones in life—the many who yearn for hope, who experience difficulty, who are sick in body and in mind and whom we can reach with a message and a demonstration that would bring the sunshine into their lives. Thus shall we qualify truly to be the ambassadors of the great, creative spirit of all life."

There is no "parliament" in the spirit world because there is no need to make laws to regulate the lives of the people who dwell there, said Silver Birch at a different sitting.

"The natural law," explained the guide, "takes care of people in the spirit world because they are confronted with it in a form which is inescapable. They no longer have physical bodies; the problem of physical life does not concern them. They are now expressing themselves in spiritual form and the natural law is in operation. There is no need for any intermediary."

The guide was asked whether there were concerts, theatres and museums in the spirit world. Their museums, he said, were "in the halls or buildings of learning where there are collections of varying kinds, of objects relating to earthly life throughout history, and also collections of interesting forms of spiritual life. For example, we have flowers that have not bloomed on earth. We have many other phases of natural life unknown to you. There are examples of these in the halls of learning.

"Concerts are always available because there are so many

musicians, many of them masters, whose desire is that their talents should be enjoyed by the largest possible number. Theatres—there are many of varying kinds. Some are used purely for dramatic purposes, others for cultural purposes, and others for educational purposes.

"Gifts, talents and faculties which people had in your world do not end with death. Death brings them greater freedom and the extended opportunities to express those talents."

"Are there newspapers and radio?" was the next question.

"No, we do not have radio because communication is differently used," explained Silver Birch. "Telepathy is the common method of reaching one another. But it is possible for those who know how, to address vast numbers and to reach them, even when they are not themselves present. But it does not work on the principle of your radio.

"There are no newspapers in your earthly sense, because there is no necessity to chronicle happenings, as you do. Information is constantly being dispensed to those who should have it by the ones whose occupation it is to spread these facts. This is difficult for you to understand.

"When it is necessary for me to be told something that I do not know the thought is sent to me by the one who thinks I ought to know it. There are people engaged on the task of disseminating these thoughts. They are specially trained for it."

"Does the same thing happen to us when we receive inspiration?" asked a member of the circle.

"It is on a different scale," began the answer. "When you receive inspiration it is because consciously or unconsciously you are tuned in to some intelligence in our world and, for that time, you are able to receive his power, inspiration or message. Sometimes it is conscious, sometimes it is unconscious. It depends upon the circumstances.

"But in our life we are constantly receiving and

transmitting thoughts. Those who are on our spiritual wavelength, that is, of like spiritual mentality, receive thoughts that we send them and transmit thoughts to us. The wavelength is determined by spiritual attainment."

"Do people retain their earth names?" was the next question. "Is Abraham Lincoln, for instance, still known as Abraham Lincoln in the spirit world?"

"Yes," said Silver Birch, "as long as it is necessary for a person to be so identified. But what you must remember is that the name is not the individual; it is only the means by which he is known."

"If someone passes on who is known to many people by a certain name, it would be very convenient for him to keep that name," observed a sitter.

"Yes," he was told, "as long as it is necessary for him or her to be so identified. That may take hundreds or even thousands of years. But once you have passed beyond the magnetic field of the earth, the name does not matter because you are then known for the individual that you truly are."

"Can that be witnessed by people?"

"Yes. Once you have got beyond the earthly pull, once you have passed the stage of earthly association and reached the span of spiritual life to which you are thus entitled, you emit a light, an aura, a radiation, which indicates who and what you are. Is that hard to understand?"

"No," said the questioner. "In our world, sometimes without speaking to a person, you are able to ascertain what kind of an individual he is."

"Yes, it is in the aura," commented Silver Birch. "It is like that here, but on a much intensified scale."

Another question was, "Do they have famous men and women in the spirit world, distinct from the famous men and women of this world?"

"Most decidedly," said the guide. "Fame comes to many

people in your world through sheer birth and for no other reason. They have not won it by their life, their endeavour, or their labour. There are many, many beings unknown, unrecognised in your world, to whom the lustre of fame is accorded in our world. The soul is the indelible passport."

"Are there books or anything equivalent in the other world?" was a further question.

"Yes, there are many, many books," said Silver Birch. "There is a duplicate of every book known to your world, and there are many other volumes of which there are no originals in your world. There are vast halls or buildings dedicated to all the arts, and literature has its place among them. It is possible to obtain knowledge of any subject in which you are interested."

"Who prepares the books?"

"Authors, people who are specialists in the task of preparing books."

"Are they etheric books which etheric people can pick up and read?"—"Yes!"

Then the discussion took one of those turns which throw new light on old problems. "Could the same book be something different to somebody else?" was the question which started it.

"No," explained the guide, who asked, "Have you ever dreamed you were reading a book?"

"I have not," was the answer, "but I can quite imagine what the experience is like."

"Would it be a real book?" asked Silver Birch. "No," he was told.

"Supposing," the guide went on, "you never woke, that dreams were your constant reality and you had no waking experience with which to compare your dream life, everything that transpired in dreams would be real to you and all that had happened in waking life would now become the shadow.

"All the mental processes utilised during the dream state are engaged in to a much greater intensity in the worlds beyond death. As those mental states are the reality of the people who dwell in those worlds, the states are as tangible to them as material things are to you in your world."

"I am appalled by the prospect," said the first questioner, who was asked by the guide, "Why?"

"It does not seem to be such a satisfactory life, bearing the hall-mark of reality which we experience here," was the answer.

"That," said the guide, "is purely a matter of comparison. Actually yours is the shadow cast by the sun of our life. Yours is the husk, yours is not the reality. Nowhere in the world of matter do you have the hall-mark of reality because matter depends on spirit for its existence. Matter is but one manifestation in one form of vibration of spiritual reality."

"I said that," replied the sitter, "because, to me, subjective beauty is not as pleasant as objective beauty."

"What you consider subjective now will be objective," explained Silver Birch, "and what you consider objective now will be subjective."

"And I suppose," commented the debater, "you have got to have personal experience of these things to appreciate them."

"You have," said Silver Birch. "But I am not so sure that you have not personal experience now."

"In dreams?"

"No, in your own mental states. You love your wife very much. Is that love subjective or objective?"

"I think it is a combination of the two."

"But love is of the spirit, soul and mind, otherwise it could not endure," replied the guide. "Reality starts from within. You are spiritual beings with material bodies. The eternal reality is the spirit, not the physical body. The spirit will endure when the body has decayed and resolved itself into the elements from which it was composed."

Once, when Silver Birch had returned from a visit "far into the recesses of the inner realms" of his world where, with many others, the task of helping humanity to gain a spiritual view of life had been reviewed, he explained that he went to gather more power for the task on which he and many others are engaged.

"It is always with a sense of flatness that I return to your world," he said, "and yet 'flatness' does not quite convey the sensation. Your world is void of all light and life. It is dull and drab and it lacks vitality. Yours is like an old cushion in which the spring has gone and everything sags. An atmosphere of gloom hangs everywhere. There are few with radiant spirits and joyful minds. There is a great feeling of spiritlessness. So very few are filled with the joy of life, and despair and indifference are on every hand. You are, perhaps, so accustomed to it that you do not notice it."

"I think we notice it as well," said a member of the circle. "The place seems full of cynicism."

Continuing his comments, the guide said: "It is the price being paid for war. You cannot have strength poured out at a fast and furious pace and be surprised at the weakness that results. There is no fire, no ardour, no enthusiasm.

"I come from a realm where all is light and colourful, where hearts sing with the sheer joy of living, where all are busily engaged in congenial pursuits, where all the arts flourish, where each is imbued with the idea of service, with sharing what he has with those who have it not, where there is the desire to instruct the uninstructed, to enlighten the less knowledgeable, where there is an intensity and vitality, a joy and radiance in well-doing.

"And here all seems such gloom. Yet this is the soil in which we must labour; this is the field in which we must serve; this is the material with which all the efforts must be made. Every individual is a part of the Great Spirit with the infinite potentialities of the Great Spirit. Each possesses within his own being the means of supplying inspiration and strength to overcome the problems of daily existence.

"Few seem to know about the eternal realities or how to call into being the finer, more beautiful faculties that they possess. So many prefer the drabness of physical existence when they could have the rich colour and zest of the spiritual life which is as real as the physical; in fact it is more real. Do you see why I feel like this?"

"Yes," said a circle member, "but isn't it true that there is another part of spirit life far more drab than our world?"

"Yes, that is true," said the guide. "There are infinite gradations of spirit life ranging from the extreme depths of despair to the heights of heavenly achievement."

"So this world would seem heaven to some of the most degraded parts," commented the sitter.

"It is always true," replied Silver Birch, "that, in comparison, there are worse and better, but I was comparing what I have seen with that to which I returned. And yet, if all these people knew what we know, they need not be cast down, their backs need not be bent. They could be uplifted, for they would realise that the source of all strength is to be found in the spirit and that the acquisition of eternal riches is more important than many of the things that cause them anxiety.

"I see so many worried, fearful, anxious over matters that need not cause the dissipation of all this energy. It is the wrong emphasis, the wrong stress. One day adjustment has to be made."

When Silver Birch mentioned that W. T. Parish, the famous healer, by then "dead," was one of two companions on his journey into the spheres, a member of the circle asked: "Is he very busy these days? Is he able to exercise his gifts?"

The guide replied: "We are always busy because there is no need to go to sleep. You cannot tire out the spirit. There is no question of recuperation involved. There is nothing to get fatigued. There is no running down or getting old or wearing out."

"You must expend energy," remarked a sitter, "some of the psychic energy that needs replenishing."

"No," replied the guide, "you are inbreathing it all the time as you are expending it. You must remember that we are not dependent upon oxygen or any gas for existence."

In an aside to his questioner, he said, "You are always puzzled by the life in the spirit world, aren't you?"

"I must confess I am," he answered. "Of course, I could blindly accept what is told to me, but perhaps it is my nature to ask questions."

"You know that I am not in favour of blind acceptance," commented the guide, who added: "There are no beds in the spirit world except for those who want them. There is no necessity for sleep because there is no night."

"Although some people do go to sleep?"

"Yes, of course, they think they ought to do so, but the enlightened ones do not go to sleep. If you want to rest on a bank, well you just rest, but not because you are tired."

"Because it is pleasant to sit and contemplate?"

"Or to exchange ideas with someone while gazing at some natural vista. But you do not say, 'Forgive me, I am tired, I must have a rest, perhaps you will not disturb me,' or 'I must hurry now to have my dinner.' There is no dinner—unless you want to eat. You are not possessed of organs that require replenishment because you are no longer in a physical vibration."

Silver Birch ended his visit with these words: "I am very happy to have the chance of making this renewal in my association. It was the thoughts of all of you that provided the warmth and the consciousness of a mission still unfulfilled.

"Much has been done, much more remains to be done.

I wish we had a magic carpet so that we could travel and visit all the people to whom it has been our privilege to give a little help. Then, with a different kind of magic carpet, we would seek all those in my world who were helped, too. Then we would realise that the work we do is much greater than appears on the surface. I do not count. I am always sincerely humble in the face of the task that is yet to be done—by all of us.

"So, hold you heads high; know that you are the instruments of a divine purpose and let your lives be so regulated that all who cross your path may realise what it is you are trying to do. Serve them wherever you can, lift them up where you can, guide them where you can. Service is all that matters, for when all else has been forgotten, when all earthly possessions have crumbled into dust, when all earthly riches have tarnished and rusted, the service you rendered will still be the imperishable jewel of your character."

'The mists of ignorance'

"I pray that the Great White Spirit shall bless our endeavours to spread knowledge and truth and wisdom and understanding as we seek to reveal the purpose and the law that is behind all life in all its varied manifestations.

"Thou hast been misunderstood and misinterpreted. Thou hast been regarded as a revengeful deity, reeking with blood, desiring sacrifices, befriending some and rejecting others, conferring boons on the few and disregarding the vast concourse of those who were turned away from Thy sight.

"We reveal that Thou art the law of life, the simple, natural, eternal, immutable law that knows no change, that operates for all eternity, that always was and that always will be.

"We seek to spread this knowledge so that it shall free men from the chains of superstition which bind them, that it may remove the blinkers from their eyes and unstop their ears and open their hearts, that they may be ready for that larger truth, that larger wisdom, that larger vision that can guide them to fulfil their divine destinies.

"We desire to abolish all the sadness and misery that is caused by the misunderstanding of natural law, to overthrow every tyranny, every vested interest and every selfishness which is an obstacle to the fulfilment of that peace and harmony which could be.

"We strive to drive away the mists of ignorance that for too long have beclouded the human vision and prevented it from perfecting a scheme of life which could bring harmony, well-being and co-operation amongst all men.

"Our power, our inspiration, our love are freely offered to all who will accept them. We make no distinction. We only strive to bring the children of earth into touch with their Father, that they call God, so that the fullness of divine power and wisdom may be theirs and may manifest in their lives so that sadness and suffering and sorrow shall be driven away and in their place there shall rule triumphantly a new knowledge, a new purpose and a new understanding."

Chapter Two

'TOWARDS THE LIGHT'

DESPITE the terrible damage inflicted on London during the second world war, the Hannen Swaffer Home Circle continued to meet. Medium Maurice Barbanell, then editor of "Psychic News," could say with justifiable pride after hostilities ceased, "We never missed a week, either." For never did the paper fail to appear. And throughout the war years, Silver Birch's words appeared regularly in "Psychic News," doubtless providing much-needed inspiration, reassurance, comfort and above all hope.

At one gathering the guide was asked how he would present spirit truths to the defeated peoples of Europe. As ever, his wise words go far beyond answering the immediate question and are as cogent today as when first spoken.

"Truth is truth," began the guide, "eternal in quality, but infinite in its variations and facts. You cannot enunciate a truth so that it can be grasped immediately by masses of people, all of them at different stages of evolution and whose soul growth would react differently to the same truth.

"I have always taught that the plan of the spirit is not to convert large numbers on one occasion, for we know that such methods produce no lasting or enduring benefit. The crowd, the mass, may be spellbound or dazzled for a while, but inevitably there is a reaction, and when they are free from all the dominance of mass psychology and begin to function as individuals, then very often there is a rueful awakening.

"No, our plan has been to reach individuals, one by one, to build on the unit, giving to them according to their spiritual needs, so that once they have established the reality of spiritual truths, taught to them in most cases by those whom they loved most in life, and who have been transferred to our world, then that conviction will remain, and all the storms and buffetings of circumstance will not disturb that solid foundation.

"So that there is no way of bringing conviction to large numbers of people, no way that would be satisfying so far as results are concerned.

"You must remember that before there can be appreciation of spiritual truths, the soul must be ready to receive them, otherwise you are trying to pierce granite. But once the soul is touched by suffering, by sorrow, the granite has gone and instead there is a far more malleable material, receptive, ready, willing to learn.

"But there is a message for all those who are oppressed. You must appeal to their reason and to the highest that is within them. It is no use calling forth the remains of their animal ancestry and encouraging them to think that their best plan is to demand an eye for an eye and a tooth for a tooth.

"They must be told that the price of their suffering should redeem them and make them fit and ready to play their part in the New World where there should be no hatred, no rancour, no bitterness, but the desire to live in mutual co-operation."

Then the discussion veered round to a familiar topic of the day, "What will the world of the United Nations do with the defeated Axis peoples?" One member of the circle, a former parson, said, "I feel I could never shake hands with one of them again."

"It is the privilege of those who have knowledge to aid those who have been misdirected," came the guide's answer. "Do not let the atmosphere of war completely blind you to the underlying eternal spiritual realities."

"But with all modesty," said the ex-parson, "I would not behave with such diabolical wickedness."

"Do not worry," replied the guide. "The law is perfect. Each receives his just portion of compensation and retribution. The Great Spirit, whose infinite intelligence planned the whole universe and devised immutable laws for its governance, has also provided for all who live in that universe and none will escape the operation of the natural law. Do not confuse vengeance with retribution.

"We approach the problem from different perspectives. You cannot fashion a world on vengeance and hatred; these cloud your judgement and make you unfit to decide or to build."

"Is not vengeance some part of retribution?" asked the sitter.

"No," was the answer. "Vengeance is the old Mosaic law, retribution is how the law of the Great Spirit works—that to each according to his deserts is given."

"Would you say," persisted the one-time minister, "that one set of men should never punish another set of men?"

And Silver Birch replied: "I would treat them as you treat those whose minds are unsound: give them the corrective treatment that will enable them to view life in its true perspective, that if you must punish—and I do not see always the need for it—then it must be that kind of punishment that will help the soul to find itself and not the kind that will encourage more hatred and breed more wars."

"If you deal lightly with such people," said the sitter, "you probably will have a recurrence of war in twenty years' time. I say get rid of them."

"How do you get rid of them?" asked the guide.

"As in this war," was the reply.

"And has that solved your problem?" was the rejoinder. "Does their influence cease to exist because their bodies no longer function? Does life only exist in your world? Do you think that thousands of souls compelled to leave their bodies filled with hatred will help your world?"

"It might teach them a lesson," was the sitter's comment. "It might teach them something different."

"It will teach them to hate," said the guide. "Hatred begets hatred, love begets love. Do not try to judge with the eyes of matter. It has been tried before and failed. When you execute a murderer, you have not solved the problem. He returns very often and inspires others to murder.

"How is the problem solved? His punishment should be remedial, to make him a fit citizen of society, to take his rightful place. His mind was diseased: you should put it right. That is the true way, the helpful way, the way of service, the way that takes cognisance of the law and works with it."

Then the guide was asked, "How would you approach two spirit beings, both having died fighting each other?"

"It depends on the two spirits," said the guide. "I am sorry to make the qualification, but these are not questions to which stock answers can be given. It depends upon the state of their progress. In some cases they go on fighting for a long time, but ultimately there comes the recognition that with the death of their bodies the enmities bred in a physical world no longer persist.

"In the lower stages of the spirit world, there is a replica of all that transpires in your physical world. All the warfare and fighting still continues, but gradually as realisation comes, the soul leaves the astral world and sheds all the prejudices and enmities that it had in your world.

"Then these problems begin to solve themselves, for with a true understanding of spiritual laws they realise that their task is to equip themselves, to perfect their own gifts, to develop their own talents, which can be achieved only by giving service. These are purely temporary problems, problems of how to bring recognition of spiritual facts to those who are not yet aware of them. All kinds of expedients have to be used.

"One of the greatest tasks is to convince those who do not believe that they have left your world. Some are obstinate, some are less obstinate, some are more receptive. The whole of mankind is not at the same stage of evolution, and therefore the approach to every soul must be according to his individual needs."

During the days when Britain was suffering from air raids, it is not surprising that an inquirer put this point to Silver Birch: "Quite a lot of your teaching relates to the casting out of fear, but this is very difficult when enemy bombs are dropping. Isn't it natural to be afraid in such circumstances?"

The guide answered: "Yes, it is; but you can also learn to cast out fear. I know that many of the ideals that we hold in front of you are not easy of attainment. It is not easy to realise all that we desire should come within your reach, but the greatest riches are usually those which are obtained after difficulty.

"These prizes require much labour. It is because they are so worth-while that I urge them upon you. I say to you that you are in part infinite spirits; the same essence of infinity that created the whole world is within each one of you.

"If you will learn how to tap that potency which is yours, if you will learn how to call upon the divine reserves that you have, if you will learn how to draw on the reservoir of the spirit, then from that armoury you can receive all that will fortify you when you feel fear.

"You have the means of conquering all that besets you in your journey through life. It is within yourself. The Nazarene put it one way, 'The kingdom of heaven is within you.' And it is a kingdom of infinite treasures you have as you develop yourself. And the higher you develop the more treasures you realise can be yours for ever.

"If it were an easy gospel we always preached, then it would mean that life had few opportunities for advancement and evolution. There are many difficulties to be overcome; that is why there is an infinity of perfection to be achieved. Life is infinite; there is no end, and the growth towards perfection is an infinite process, too."

At another sitting, Silver Birch spoke on a different aspect of fear when he was asked the following question: "Allowing for exaggeration, there does undoubtedly exist, in some, a reluctance for physical combat amounting to what is termed cowardice. If more members of the human race were similarly affected wars would become rarer. How does the spirit world view this?"

"It is a natural expression of the individual," the guide's answer began. "I always teach that life is in contrasts, that hatred is love inverted, that fear is bravery inverted. They are all the same qualities, expressed at different ends of the pole of emotion. I always have said that as correspondingly low that you can sink, so correspondingly high can you rise.

"Fear can be transmuted into courage, hatred can be transmuted into love. Some may find that a difficult gospel to accept. That is what I teach. The mind embraces a variety of complex emotions and feelings. If you apply yourself to controlling them you evolve and you grow, and the lower is transmuted into the higher."

"Is it a bad thing to be a coward?" the guide was asked.

"I say it is not bad or good," Silver Birch replied. "It is natural because it is an emotion, a feeling which is part of your equipment. Because you have mind, you have all the qualities of mind, whether you express them outwardly or not, they are still there.

"Bravery and cowardice are part of your mental and spiritual equipment. You may not show them, but they are still there. You may feel them without expressing them outwardly, but they are still there. What I am striving to teach is that, however negative or undesirable are these qualities, you have the power to transmute them into their higher aspects, which to me is the most important lesson. Cowardice is exactly of the same quality as courage. It is its inversion, and you can, with all the power that you possess, transmute it."

"Do you call it a negative attribute, in the same way as hate?" the guide was asked.

"Yes, I do," was the answer. "I say it is part of the mind's equipment. The mind possesses all attributes."

Asked to comment on the questioner's statement, "If more people were cowards, in other words, negative, there would be no war," Silver Birch said: "That is not so. It is quite obvious that war is not solved by turning everybody into cowards."

Then, at another meeting of the circle, Silver Birch spoke as he did more than once on the subject of suffering, saying:

"Suffering is part of the law. Even those who are victims of suffering, though they may dislike it, suffer because they have broken the law. It is part of the law, and if you did not suffer you would not learn."

"But suffering is not the only way of development," a sitter commented.

"Of course not," said Silver Birch, "but it is one of the important ways. I cannot understand those who want to flinch from hardship or danger or difficulty.

"If you are to gain your goal, if you are to perfect all your gifts, you must go through fire, you must be tried and tested, otherwise who knows what is your mettle?"

Somebody present said: "People have got the idea of a benevolent deity, and development of character through suffering is foreign to them."

"Who said the Deity is benevolent?" challenged the guide. "The Deity is law, benevolent in its ultimate, but the law sends sunshine and the rain, the law sends snow and the storm, the law sends calm and the storm, the law sends the heat and the cold, the law is in everything.

"I have tried to teach that through love and hatred, through anger and passion, it is the supreme law. But many have disagreed with me. They could not understand how the Great Spirit could be in hatred. But the Great Spirit, being the Great Spirit, must exist in everything. It is the law, the perfect law."

"If everybody perfectly adhered to the law," said a member of the circle, "they would see the benevolence."

"Of course, but the processes are eternal," said the guide. "One day you will not see through a glass darkly. You will realise that those were the most important lessons of your life and that if you had not suffered you would not have understood. It is a hard lesson to learn, but it is a lesson. If all lessons were easy, if there were no hardships, no temptations, no difficulties, if life were one long pleasure cruise, the race would become moribund."

Similar themes were discussed at a later seance, when Silver Birch said:

"There is none who goes through your earthly life free from pain and suffering, toil and anguish, whose life is lived for ever in the sunshine, who has none of the shadows. I know of no such case."

The guide had been asked, "If suffering is necessary to develop one's character, doesn't it seem to be a form of injustice that some people don't suffer?"

He answered: "Who said so? Suffering is not always an outward sign that is visible to the casual onlooker. Suffering is what the heart and mind and soul feel within. Do not attempt to judge mankind by the mask it wears in its daily life. It is the soul that feels and registers."

Then the sitter who had put the question asked, "If

suffering is so important and essential to the evolution of character, why do you continually urge that everything should be done for the alleviation of suffering?"

"Of course, I do," replied Silver Birch, "but I am not foolish enough to imagine that you will ever have a world in which there were no suffering of any kind, in which perfection has been reached. I realise that life is infinite in its progress. Therefore, to attain all the steps of infinite progress you have to evolve all the time, and evolution means the gradual perfecting of that which was imperfect—and that must be a painful process.

"But at the same time, I recognise that there is much needless suffering, the suffering that is self-inflicted, the suffering that is caused by wilful ignorance and deliberate stupidity, the suffering that comes from prejudice, the suffering that comes from rigid alliance with superstition. It is all that needless suffering that I want to see abolished. But because man is an evolving being, he will always be struggling towards the light. All processes of birth are usually accomplished by struggle.

"The trouble is that so many of them feel very sorry for themselves, and they do not realise that when they can view their early life dispassionately, when they can judge themselves apart from the circumstances which at present colour the whole of their thinking, then they will see that the greatest progress was made at the time when all seemed dark, drear and difficult.

"The realisation comes in the hours of bitterness. If there were never any pain, if there were never any anguish, if there were never any heartaches, the soul would hardly be aware of itself or its innate capabilities."

Another sitter asked: "Why do you say you improve by suffering or that you develop? Why is it that in some cases it either improves a person or destroys their character?"

"Then the real character has not emerged," replied Silver Birch. "The aspect which exhibited itself before was just as unreal as the aspect which exhibits itself after the suffering. The reality has yet to emerge."

Another question was, "Why should some people be spiritually gifted and not others?"

"All the gifts of the spirit are possessed by every being potentially," said the guide. "That must be so because they are spiritual beings, but in some there are certain gifts that lie nearer the surface and are therefore capable of development. You might as well ask me: 'Why are some endowed with beauty of form and others are not? Why are some endowed with talent to paint and others are not?' There is an explanation, but that involves going into some intricate problems."

Somebody else asked: "We hear of the sea being calm at Dunkirk and of the weather being favourable at Sicily. Was this due to divine intervention?"

"There is no intervention by the Great Spirit," replied the guide. "The laws, the universal natural laws, have always been in existence—and will always be in existence. There is no circumstance that has ever happened, or that will ever happen, that requires the suspension of any natural law or the intervention in any natural law.

"The world is ruled by natural laws, and it is not necessary for any interference to take place. If it were, then the Great Spirit would cease to be the Great Spirit, for, instead of being perfect, the Great Spirit would be chaotic."

"I asked that," said a member of the circle, "because many eminent people speaking on the wireless recently seemed to think that divine providence has been on our side."

And the guide answered: "To me eminence is only achieved by greatness of soul. I know of no other standard of judgement. And do not allow your nation, however just its cause, to imagine that the Great Spirit takes sides. The Great Spirit is the law.

"If you do that which is right, then automatically you place yourself in harmony with the operation of natural law. There is no need to visualise a magnified human deity who summons all the forces just to aid you in your hour of difficulty. And that, too, includes a lot of Spiritualists who still think in terms of a personal God."

"I suppose," said the sitter, "everybody is in a different stage of evolution and it is difficult for them to understand."

"I do not mind when they disagree with me or tell me how wrong or misguided I am," responded Silver Birch. "I can only express the truth as I see it, and as I have learnt it after many long years of evolution.

"If that upsets their ideas of religion, or Christianity, or Hinduism, I cannot help it. I am not concerned with labels, with creeds, or with any concepts of religion. I am concerned only with the truth as I have learned it. That is my only standard of judgement.

"I ask no souls to accept what I say if it seems unreasonable to them. I state what I know as humbly, as sincerely, as reverently as I can. I lay all my knowledge, all the wisdom I have acquired at the feet of those who will accept it. If they decide to reject it, that is their responsibility; it is not mine."

'Shadows cross the sky'

"I would like to give a message to all those people who read my words and say that I succeed in giving them comfort, all those whose lives were lonely and who have now been able to realise that in truth they are not alone but encompassed by a wealth of love from the realm of spirit.

"I am grateful if I have succeeded in touching any one

heart, in opening the eyes of any one individual, enabling the owner to find that truth which brings freedom to the soul.

"I rejoice wherever ignorance is driven out, wherever superstition retreats, wherever bigotry vanishes, wherever intolerance fades away.

"I rejoice wherever the power of the spirit is made manifest and love finds its own, even when it has to penetrate the barriers of death itself.

"I rejoice wherever knowledge comes into its own and men and women learn that there is a Great Spirit filled with love towards them, Whose laws when properly understood by them enable them to find a richness which the world of matter cannot give them or even take away from them.

"And to all who send me silent thoughts, and all who send me love, to all who send me petitions which, alas, I cannot answer, I express my gratitude, and only ask that I shall continue to serve them, to lead them always on the paths that bring them nearer to an understanding of His laws, His power and His peace.

"We turn our eyes to the path of rich promise, knowing that the road we tread will give service to many who need it.

"Shadows cross the sky, the light wanes. Soon the stars glitter and the pale light of the moon is reflected in the heavens. Darkness descends, night envelops the world in her mantle. But soon the sun rises and the glory of its radiance is beheld.

"In truth the sun has never ceased to shine, for its light is there even when not seen in the world of matter. Though you may not see all the operations of the Law, the Law is constant, the Law is immutable.

"And to the Great Spirit we turn always, Thou Who hast always been, Thou Who always will be. We pray that a fuller understanding of Thee and of Thy laws shall come into all our lives, so that we shall express to the full the richness and beauty of that divinity which is immanent within each one of us."

Chapter Three

'KNOWLEDGE BRINGS JOY'

OVER the years Silver Birch has won—and continues to win—the love, respect and admiration of countless millions in many lands throughout the world. Yet two of his greatest followers were children, Ruth and Paul Harris who, from the age of eight and six, enjoyed the privilege of a special sitting with the guide at least once a year, usually around Christmas time.

Their father Paul, a Fleet Street journalist and well-known Spiritualist author, was a close friend of Maurice Barbanell. So it was that Paul, and his wife Fay, raised their children with a knowledge of the spiritual realm's reality.

The youngsters generally prepared a list of questions to be put to the Other-Side mentor . . . and no help or suggestions regarding the points to be raised were accepted from adults! Here is Paul Harris' account of one such seance:

Two children stood beside Silver Birch, the wise old spirit guide of Hannen Swaffer's Home Circle, and as they in turn said goodbye because he was about to depart for his sojourn in the spheres, he said, first to Ruth, "Grow in grace and strength, love and wisdom." And to the boy, Paul, he said: "Be strong and confident and know that the power of the spirit is behind you. Always with the strength of my being, with the love of my heart and the wealth of my spirit I will strive to serve you."

Those are the words, but they do not convey anything of the warmth of the affection between these three who have met every year for six years, the children to ask questions about the spirit world, and the guide to answer them. For an hour and twenty minutes the children, who take it very seriously, had asked questions and discussed the answers. They are young people now, and have grown to regard Spiritualism as part of their lives.

For days they had discussed the questions to be asked and refused all adult suggestions. The questions began.

Ruth: "I would like to know whether the way you die has any effect when you reach the spirit world; whether, if you die just naturally, it is easier to get to the spirit world or not?"

Silver Birch: "Oh, yes, it makes a very big difference. If everyone in your world had knowledge and lived natural lives—I said 'if'—then the process of what is called dying would be simple and free from any pain. Also, it would be unnecessary to have any adjustments to the body of the spirit after the physical body has died. But unfortunately that does not take place.

"The vast majority of those who leave your world for ours are profoundly ignorant of their destiny, of their own constitution and of the nature of spiritual realities. In addition, there are far, far too many who come to us before their time is ripe, and as I so often say, they are like the fruit which drops from the tree before it is ready—as you know, then the fruit is not very good.

"When fruit is ripe it drops naturally, and when your spirit is ripe, the physical body should naturally drop away from you. And so we have today sour and green fruit coming to us. Because of that they have to be tended, watched over, cared for, nursed, until the adjustments are made. If all had knowledge, then the work of those who like myself are striving to help would be far easier. Certainly it makes a tremendous difference to the way you die. Does that answer it?"

Ruth: "Yes, I think you have answered it very well and very clearly."

Paul: "I know the Indian races very often had people who were able to bring rain by performing some ceremony, or doing something. What has the spirit world got to do with this? Has it got anything to do with it?"

Silver Birch: "No. There is a difference between knowledge of psychic laws and knowledge of spiritual laws. They are not entirely the same. People speak of astral and spiritual as if the two words could be exchanged, but they do not mean the same thing at all.

"Now, the Indian races were instructed in many of the psychic laws which are concerned with the physical phenomena of your world. I mean the purely physical phenomena, and the ability to induce the elements to come within the local range of their ceremonies was something that was well known to the skilled and practised medicine man.

"You know, it is a very difficult question to answer simply, but it had nothing really to do with the spirit world; it had more to do with the psychic laws that are concerned with the physical phenomena of your earth. I do not think I have made that clear, have I?"

Paul: "Yes, except what sort of laws do you mean?"

Silver Birch: "Oh, you want to go and do it?"

A member of the circle, breaking the rule that grown-ups should not speak until near the end, asked, "Would it be something the same as psychometry, not necessarily proving spiritual laws?"

Silver Birch: "I can give plenty of illustrations, but I am bearing in mind that they should be well understood. Take, for example, the clairvoyant. Now, there are many people in your world who are clairvoyant, but who have no contact with the spirit world. Their clairvoyance is part of their psychic make-up, and because of that they can touch psychic laws and see with their psychic eyes; but there is no one from the spirit world connected with that demonstration. They do not even see the dead. They see scenes; they have premonitions; they can see sometimes into the future and into the past. Now all that can happen, but there is no touch with the spirit world at all. It is purely the natural psychic faculty of the clairvoyant. Is that quite clear?"

"That is something I should not have thought happened," said the children's mother. "I should not have thought that a clairvoyant giving evidence or seeing psychic things could do it without being in actual touch with the spirit world."

Silver Birch: "Nevertheless, it is so, that many of you can exercise a psychic faculty now and have exercised the psychic faculty on the physical plane. It is an extension of the five senses. It does not touch the world of spirit at all. It does touch the psychic laws or the psychic factors which surround the physical laws. In much the same way as the fortune-teller, the genuine fortune-teller, or the genuine crystal-gazer can see and hear without any spirit intervention, so the medicine man, skilled in the use of his own psychic faculties, could harmonise those faculties by means of certain ceremonies and rituals with the power behind the physical law and produce rain. That is the clearest I can put it."

"That is very clear," said a sitter. "It is rather a fascinating subject to have touched on, because I find myself just wondering how far one could go."

Silver Birch: "Quite a long way. In India there are many yogis who are very skilled, but they have no contact with the world of spirit. Many of them would be terrified if they saw a spirit."

"If they saw a spirit, they would describe a spirit," said another sitter.

Silver Birch: "Then you are touching quite a different vibration. All mediumship is a co-operation of the spiritual and the psychic, and it is in the blending of the power that you have spirit communication. The ability to communicate with our world does not depend wholly on the psychic faculty of the instrument, but in the co-operation of a spirit guide or control with an instrument."

Paul: "I am sorry to be so dense, but I am not quite sure what is the difference between psychic and spiritual. I thought they were the same."

Silver Birch: "Almost the same, but not quite. You can have all the psychic faculties, but they do not become spiritual faculties until they are used for a spiritual purpose in association with spiritual people in our world. You are naturally psychic, as well as physical, and you all have the faculties of the psychic body, but it is not until these faculties are developed and blended with the power of the spirit that they become spiritual gifts."

Paul: "Could you tell us the difference in the levels of the astral plane? You are always talking about different levels. What are the actual differences in these levels?"

Silver Birch: "They are differences in growth, but they cannot be measured in any physical sense. If I say to you what is the difference in measurement between a fool and a wise man, or what is the difference between a miser and a saint, there is no answer, is there?

"But there is a tremendous difference in the growth of their spirits. In our life you occupy just that sphere to which you have grown, that is, the sphere with which you harmonise because your mental, moral and spiritual growth determine it. The difference is purely the difference of the people who live there. The higher you are spiritually, the better you are, the kinder you are, the more charitable you are, the more unselfish you are, the higher is the level on which you live in your world.

"But because you are all on the same physical level, it does not mean that you are on the same mental level or on the same spiritual level. Your bodies are on the same level, but once the body, the physical body, has gone, you live at the level of your spiritual growth."

Paul: "Yes, I see. I would just like to ask you something more. Is this earth just one of these levels, or something apart from the usual?"

Silver Birch: "No, the world is part of the astral world because all worlds are interpenetrating. All stages of life throughout the whole of the universe mingle and merge into one another and spiritual, astral, physical are varying aspects of one universal life. At this very moment you are registering in the physical world, in the astral world and in the spiritual world all at the same time."

Ruth: "I thought instead of Paul and I asking you questions that you would tell us something because you know so much more than we, and some things we would not dream of thinking you might tell us."

Silver Birch: "Yes, I will, but does that finish all your questions?"

Ruth: "No. I would like to know whether being brought up as a Spiritualist has made any difference to me or to Paul?"

Silver Birch: "What do you think?"

Ruth: "Well, I can't tell, can I? I cannot tell what difference it has made to me because I am not in the spirit world, am I?"

Silver Birch: "No, and yes."

Ruth's mother added: "She does not know what it is to be brought up without Spiritualism and she cannot compare. You can see both sides."

Silver Birch: "I can see it even with the eyes closed. I only say, 'What do you think?' because you know so many other children who do not have this knowledge. Do you think they are worse or better?"

Ruth: "Well, they are worse in the sense that they won't be prepared when they are going to the spirit world. They are lacking that knowledge and experience, but apart from that I really don't know. I am sorry."

Paul: "I agree with Ruth in the first thing. I don't think there is any difference. When you die you know what is going to happen, but apart from that I don't see what difference it is going to make."

Silver Birch: "The answer is very simple; that all knowledge should make a difference. Unfortunately it does not always do so. Knowledge brings joy, happiness, serenity, but it also brings responsibility as to what you do with that knowledge.

"Knowledge will drive away many of the foolish fears that come with ignorance; knowledge will make you aware of yourself and what you should do now that you know, and you know that others are less fortunate. He who sins in ignorance pays the price, but he who sins with knowledge pays a greater price, for his knowledge has increased his sin.

"So you are better off, but it depends on yourself as to what you do."

"You can't argue with that, can you?" said a member of the circle.

Silver Birch: "You know, I cannot change the law. I can only expound it. So many times I have wished I could stand in your places and receive on my own frame the blows of fate and shield you from all adversity, to be a barrier between the snows and the cold and the rains. But I cannot, for they are part of that same universal force which provides the light, the heat and the sunshine. You cannot have one without the other, for thus it is your spirits grow, through testing and by experience."

Ruth: "I really think it is very good that you can't do that, because with you to shield everybody from their troubles they would always rely on somebody else."

Paul: "There would not be any point in life."

Silver Birch: "I know, but one day you will know what it is to love with the whole of your being, and to see the one you love hurt and be unable to do anything about it.

"Now I want to add something to what I said before, and this is to you, Ruth. The overwhelming difference is the knowledge that you are never alone, that you know love and friendship and comradeship and all the warmth of the spirit accompany you wherever you may be; the knowledge that there is a guiding power that will help you whenever you put forth your best effort, the sense of presences friendly, helpful, kindly, who desire that you shall extract the best from your own being and the best from your own life. That is what this knowledge gives you, and those who do not possess it are less fortunate than you."

Paul: "Why is it that men always seem to have overruled women throughout the ages? What is the reason for this?"

Silver Birch: "Because the women have been very foolish."

Paul: "Do you think they could alter it?"

Silver Birch: "There is no necessity to alter it, for it is the women who have been ruling the men all the time."

"You did not think of it that way," said a member of the circle.

Silver Birch: "No, but there is some basis for it. It is the survival of the old days when the man was the hunter, the provider, when it was the man who built the home and had to bring food; the man who was the dominant influence, and the wife who attended him when he was tired and fed him when he was hungry. Because the male was active and the female passive, gradually all laws gave a bias in favour of the man. But this is slowly changing as more and more your world realises that neither is superior to the other, but that each is complementary."

Paul: "I see. Thank you very much."

Silver Birch: "You know I have been with you a long time,

and I have watched with interest the growth of your own minds and souls, and have seen two small trees growing straight and upright, and I rejoice that you live in an atmosphere of growing knowledge and understanding.

"There is still much to be learned, but at least you are facing the world armed with some truth, realising some of its purposes, and you know that whatever you are doing, where there is sincerity, there you will not fail. I am very close to you and help you as much as I can.

"I am very glad to have had you here today, Ruth and Paul, for I like to talk with you and to try to show you how near I am all the time. I am not far away. I am in your home, in your school, in your play. I see many things that make me laugh, but I learn the ways of your world and it helps me. I never finish learning because I am fascinated by the manners and customs of your western world."

"We often think of you," said the mother, "when we have got a nice fire and are burning some logs. We sit around and think how you like a fire and the flames."

Silver Birch: "I always warm myself in the love of those who are close to me. Love is the atmosphere which I can imbibe. Love is the great consolation I have for the joys that I miss. If you had tasted the beauties of spirit life as they exist in spheres supernal, if you had had the riches of the spheres at your disposal, you would not welcome this cold, grey world filled with rancour and bitterness, strife, hatred, bloodshed and misery.

"The compensation is the love kindled in hearts that welcome you. It is not easy to work amongst you. There are so many whose hearts are filled with stone, whose minds are distorted and who are inaccessible to wisdom, to guidance and to the love of even their own. Do you not realise how much it helps to feel kinship and sympathy, comradeship and good fellowship from those who offer you their love? You help me more than you know. You provide the means by which I can reach many others.

"Let us then constantly dwell on the poor, wayward ones of your world, misdirected, having lost their way, yearning for some touch of sympathy, for some direction, for some word of comfort and hope, for all seems bereft in their pathetic despair. These are the ones we must strive to bring within the radiance of spirit power, so that we can transform all their weary sadness and bring the light of hope and the touch of knowledge into their beings.

"As you know, I am going to leave you for a while. I go with regrets, but yet it is always necessary to return as far as possible to be recharged with that power which cometh from on high, to take counsel with others, to learn of failures and successes, to hear whether we have acquitted ourselves well or badly. I shall take with me your love and I shall leave my love in your care. I shall look forward with great anticipation to the time when I can return.

"And now let us pause to attune ourselves to the highest force in the universe, the force of which we are ourselves an integral part. Let us be conscious of the inflow, the divine power, the benediction of the breath of the spirit; let us be worthy of the highest; let us never fail in the trust reposed in us; let us so live and think and speak that we are indeed the instruments of the higher purpose; and let nothing sully in any way that sacred mission.

"Let us discharge with honour all that is laid upon our shoulders and let us face with unflinching resolve all that the future may bring, knowing that those who desire to serve are at one with the Great Spirit of life whose protection is as immeasurable as is His love."

Another time young Paul asked Silver Birch about God.

"There seem to be lots of ways in which men have expressed God," said the lad, "all different, but none very satisfactory."

"That is true," answered the guide without a moment's pause. "What you have to remember is that men are subject to growth, that they are always enlarging the horizon of their minds. Boundaries are constantly being removed. All the advances of knowledge bring a greater understanding of the universe and that which it contains.

"In the early times, when men knew little about their surroundings, when they had no understanding of the natural phenomena of life and thought them all due to the activities of gods, they could think of these gods only in terms of magnified human beings. And so you had the original idea of sacrifice. They thought that when the thunder rolled and the lightning flashed that the gods were angry and that the way to subdue that wrath was to make offerings to them.

"Gradually these crude conceptions gave way to larger ideas, and man, as he struggled, groping towards the light, emerging from the darkness of ignorance through the mists of superstition towards the dawn of knowledge, realised that the cause, the great cause, was something far beyond his imagination. But ancient ideas die hard, and this picture of a magnified man, a person who created the universe, has persisted for centuries.

"Now we come along and we say that the divine architect, the supreme ruler of the universe, is not a man, not a woman, not a being at all. It is not a person. The universe is ruled by laws, and these laws are infinite in their scope and application. They are the result of divine love and wisdom, perfect, unfailing, never subject to error or to mistake.

"Spirit is infinite, without beginning, without end; spirit cannot be compressed into matter; matter is but a poor reflection of spirit. People who live in a material world, compelled to think of everything that happens in terms of the five senses—sight, touch, smell, feeling and hearing—cannot possibly comprehend the essence of all life which is beyond these five senses.

"You cannot in any way, whilst you are subject to this limitation, understand that which is beyond limitation. So it comes to this: we say there is a universe ruled by natural laws, that the intelligence behind the laws is perfect, but that man cannot comprehend that perfection because he is imperfect. Man, being personal, cannot understand the impersonal. I hope that helps you because it is not an easy subject.

"Each one of you, all the human beings, not only on your planet but on millions of other planets, helps to constitute what I call the Great Spirit, others call God, for the Great Spirit is the sum total of all spirit that is in the universe. That is not hard to understand?"

"Don't you think," said Ruth, "that as man progresses he gets more complicated ideas of God, and the more complicated his mind gets, the further he grows away from the truth?"

"Not if he is really progressing," said the guide. "What does happen is that sometimes there is a development of the brain, but not a development of the mind or the spirit, and then you have people who are intellectual, but it does not follow that because they are intellectual they are great souls or that they have great minds.

"It is a progress that is limited strictly to the physical thing, the brain, and sometimes it is true that amongst those people there are those who reject anything but the complicated. But where there is true progress, the progress of the mind and the soul, then that progress brings a greater awareness of spiritual realities, for it is a mental and spiritual development. In those cases you get a discarding of the former erroneous conceptions and a closer approximation to the truth.

"You must always remember that it is impossible for the whole of the Great Spirit, which is infinite, to be explained in language which is finite and therefore limited. You cannot put the larger into the smaller; that must be clear. Has that helped you, Paul? Now, what are the other problems?"

"What do you think is the greatest discovery man has made?" asked Ruth, who had thought much about her question, trying to see if she could guess the answer.

"Of course, that is a difficult question to answer because of the word greatest," said Silver Birch, "and you have to ask yourself about greatness from which point of view—physical, mental or spiritual.

"In my view, the greatest discovery is the discovery by man that he was man, his discovery of his own consciousness, his awareness of himself, the realisation that he had the power, puny though he was, to know what was going on around him, for that has led him to all other discoveries. Once he knew he had a mind and had stumbled on the truth of his own potentiality, that led to all the other discoveries that have since been made.

"Man's awareness of himself means that man had realised that he was something more than a body, something more than matter, something more than a physical vessel which was subject to decay, that would crumble and be resolved into the material elements out of which he was formed. That, I think, must constitute the greatest discovery."

This answer was a surprise to the young questioners, who had thought the guide would refer to some invention.

"If you asked me what is *my* greatest discovery, that is another question," said Silver Birch.

"May we ask you that?" said Paul eagerly. "Please tell us."

"My greatest discovery," began Silver Birch, "has been to find that there is so much good will, affection, comradeship and even love within so many human beings; that if you can make the right appeal you can call this love from their natures; that they respond to the highest; that they are capable of noble deeds, noble thoughts; that they can be touched by something greater than that of self-interest; that ideas of idealism, altruism and service will call forth a response.

"I think of the many years that I have worked in this cold, grey, unattractive, sombre world of yours, and then see how warmth has come into it because of love that has been kindled in many hearts by people who do not know me, but who love me because they say I have helped them. I never expected to win so much love, and it is a source of gratification to me, one that inspires me and makes me feel unworthy, for I realise that I have never done that which would justify it."

That was something which they did not expect, and it encouraged them to put more questions. Paul asked, "What changes have occurred in the world since you were here, and what changes have happened in the spirit world in the same time?"

Again without pausing, the guide replied: "Very largely, in the world of matter, the change that has come over the scene is what is known as the process of civilisation. Man has made tremendous strides in material things. He has learned how to harness so many of the elements of nature; he has scaled peaks and plumbed depths; he has travelled continents and oceans; he has come to the heights of physical attainments. It has been a remarkable material development. But mentally and spiritually, there has not been a similar evolution. Man has physically outstripped the growth of his mind and his soul. They have not kept pace with his material development. And there you have the dreadful results in selfishness, which is the great besetting sin of your world.

"Now, the lesson that has to be learned from that is that man cannot live in peace and enjoy all the fruits of his own being, of his own creation, unless there is a development on spiritual and mental lines that is at least some reflection of the development that has taken place on physical lines. Until that is done you must have chaos, disorder, disharmony. It is development of the mind and the spirit that will dictate the motive and inspire all the other activities into fields of co-operation and service.

"The development of the mind and the spirit will destroy selfishness; it will teach the lessons of the spirit. And when man has unfolded the talents of his mind and his spirit, and used all the physical developments, not for his own sake, but for the service of all, then, indeed, you will have achieved the kingdom of heaven on earth. For each throughout the world of matter has some talent to give which could help others less fortunate.

"As to the changes in the world of spirit that is a far, far more difficult story to try to tell. Very briefly, the great development has been the way in which the organisation responsible for building the bridges of communication has become more and more elaborate, and the plans that have been devised and carried out for ensuring that never again will the world of matter be cut off from the world of spirit without there being a sufficient number of channels through whom the power of the spirit can be made manifest. I do not think I can say any more than that."

"We are very glad to know one of the biggest tasks has been accomplished in the spirit world and that the lines of communication are well laid and plans going satisfactorily," was a comment. "That must mean a lot of good mediums are wanted in this world, and they are sadly lacking."

"The instruments will come," said Silver Birch, "the power of the spirit will continue to pour out its benefactions through many channels and in increasing number. Do not let anyone tell you that what has been achieved in the past represents the peak of attainment. It is not so. More is being achieved today than was yesterday, and more will be achieved tomorrow than is being achieved today. That is the lesson of progress, and we progress, too.

"There are always those who say, 'Who is to come after us?' When your tasks are done others will fill your shoes and the power of the spirit will continue to flow in a greater measure than it is flowing today. None can stop it."

"Has there ever been as good communication between the spirit world and this earth as there has been through Spiritualism?" asked Ruth.

"It has been in bursts of inspiration which have been occasional but not sustained," was the answer. "Now it is organised, harnessed, controlled, regulated. It is all part of one vast plan, a plan that is far more co-ordinated than you can ever realise. The organisation that is behind communication is massive and worked out in masterly detail. It has all been arranged. When it was decided to open the doors of the spirit world it was done deliberately, so that once the doors were opened they could never be closed again."

"Could you tell us some things we do when we sleep?" asked Ruth.

"Every night you leave your physical bodies behind," began the guide. "Your experiences are divided into two kinds. One is instructional, and the other is purely entertainment. On the instructional side, you are taught about the equipment of your spiritual body which will come in very handy in the years that are yet to unfold. On the entertainment side, you visit many of the halls of activity to see what is going on.

"Now, last night, Ruth, you were taken to see some of the gardens in our world, and Paul was taken to the hall of music."

"Isn't it a shame we cannot remember?" commented Paul.

"Yes, I know," said Silver Birch, "but that is the same trouble as in the first question. You are trying to put an out-of-the-body experience into a bodily understanding. The glass cannot hold all that is in the jug, but if you watch your dreams you will get very valuable clues."

"How must we account for dreams without sense and reason?" was another question.

"Do you mean distortions?" said Silver Birch. "They are the result of the attempt of the brain to remember. The brain is like a little bag. When your spirit returns, and the bag tries to capture the whole of the experience, it cannot get into the bag, and in the process of trying to cram it all in it gets all out of shape. Your dream is not a transcription of what occurred, but a memory of what occurred."

"We would like to know what we can do to help you in your work," said young Paul.

"Give me your love always," was the reply. "Trust me, send me thoughts of good will. Those are my food and drink. I only want love, good will. If I can earn those I am happy. But don't you worry about my work. I can take care of it."

Then followed a digression begun by a sitter, who said that children seemed to follow spirit teaching more easily than their parents. Silver Birch answered, "I cannot help that, but I will be a good influence on those who have their whole manhood and womanhood in front of them.

"I cannot say to you," he said to his young friends, "that life will be all sunshine. There will be shadows; rain will sometimes beat down upon you. You will have difficulties; you will meet with trials. Life is not one long monotone; it is full of colour, variety. You will meet with obstacles. You will have good moments when all seems well and other times when all seems hopeless. That is how character grows, in the variety of experiences of which life is composed.

"If the whole of life were easy, if there were no difficulties to conquer, no trials to master, no obstacles to overcome, then there would be no development. The race is worth running because it is a race. The prize is worth receiving because it is received, not with ease, but after you have deserved it. Deserve it! There is no worry that you cannot defeat; therefore do not worry. There is no difficulty which you cannot conquer; there is nothing that can happen to you that is beyond your power to overcome.

"Learn the lesson from every experience. If it seems hard, do not flinch but steel yourself, and you will be stronger as a result. Remember always that you are spirits manifesting through bodies, and that nothing which happens, nothing, can harm or hurt your eternal spirit. You must say to yourself, 'I am part of the Great Spirit; part of His divinity is within me and part of His divine strength is at my disposal when I want it.' In hours of weakness call on that strength and it will help you.

"It does not matter if you become what the world calls successful—the prizes of physical success are so easily tarnished. What does matter is that you should be loyal to the highest of your own spiritual natures, never to deny that which you know to be true, to be faithful to yourselves, to obey your conscience. Then, whatever the world may think, you will know that you have done the best you can. And when the time comes to say farewell to earth, you will do so knowing that you are ready for what awaits you. That is my advice."

At a different circle meeting, Silver Birch gave his views on children's religious education. He told those present:

"Let us begin with the very obvious truism that the child of today is the man or woman of tomorrow. Thus we realise quite simply that all the education it receives should be an adequate preparation for the life which lies ahead beyond schooling, so that it is equipped, ready to face the tasks that citizenship imposes upon all adult lives.

"True education should consist in the dissemination of that

knowledge which will enable children to be citizens of the world in which they live. It should instruct them in all the natural laws of the universe. It should make them aware of all the faculties with which they have been endowed, so that an unfolding of them will be of the greatest service to their own lives and to the world in which they live.

"The child is malleable; its mind is as yet unformed in judgement; it has no instinctive means of reflection and judgement, of weighing up whether statements which are taught are true, are false, or contain but a portion of truth. The mind of the child is very plastic, and, being trusting, it accepts as truth that which is inculcated into its mind at an age when it is too early to question the instructions which are given.

"Thus you are dealing with very precious and very delicate material, for you are helping to form impressions that will become part of the warp and the woof of the child's own being. You are reaching the subconscious mind of the child, and everything which is being taught to it will colour its thinking in later life. Those who, for whatever reason, deliberately inculcate doctrines which are false, are guilty of a very grave disservice to the future of the race and of civilisation.

"If you are ignorant of the child's many potentialities, if you are unfamiliar with spiritual realities, and, as a consequence, are unable to teach it the truths about its own being, its own nature, its relationship to the Great Spirit, its relationship to the vast cosmic plan of life, then the child will be handicapped. It will go through life not as fully equipped and armed with knowledge as it should.

"It does not fall within my province to deal with the essential requirements for the physical life. These are well known, for it is obvious that there should be tuition in all the sciences and the natural phenomena of life, in all that would help to cultivate the mind to appreciate the riches of literature and all the arts and refinements of your world.

"And so I come to the question of religion, which, seeking to give guidance to the soul so that it can be prepared to face and to conquer in all life's battles, obviously plays a paramount part in education. Because every child is part of the Great Spirit, because it is in essence a spiritual being, it is intended to live with all the benefits that freedom brings. If you cramp, if you restrict the soul of the child at an early age, you are denying it its elementary rights of freedom; you are condemning it to serfdom; you are making it a spiritual slave.

"Freedom is the essence of all education. As I see it, the child will grow in freedom if it is taught the truths about religion. If those who are teachers give instructions based upon a desire, not to give the child freedom, but to teach it loyalty to ancient myth and fable, then they are poisoning the springs of the child's mind. No service is rendered to religion, to education or to the child by teaching it discarded creeds which, if it is intelligent, it will reject at the earliest possible age.

"Then there will come the inevitable reaction. It will turn its back on all those whom it considers misled it at a time when it had no means of resisting them. The young sapling is intended to grow stalwart and straight as a tree, but if you give it nurture which is false, then you are helping to tamper with the very roots of its being and the growth will become stunted.

"We oppose all those whose desire is not to teach the truths about the spirit, not to teach about the relationship between all spiritual beings and the Great Spirit of life, but whose desire is to strengthen their tottering churches and to fill their emptying pews. The truth about religion is that no religion possesses the whole of truth. Each has seen but a glimpse and that, alas, has become distorted with the centuries or falsified by the creedalists.

"The child must be taught that true religion is to give service, to ignore all the elaborate phrase-making of priestcraft, and to live an honest, unselfish life, desiring to help the world in which it dwells and so be true to the Great Spirit of Whom it is an integral part."

'To help the fallen'

"Oh Great White Spirit, we turn to Thee, for Thou art the supreme law behind all life, Thou art the divine architect Who has fashioned the universe and has set in motion the eternal laws which control and regulate every process, every phase, every motion throughout the whole of this universe.

"Thine is the mind which has devised the law, Thine is the love which has sustained it. All begins with Thee, and all that exists owes its origin to Thee, for Thy spirit permeates all, forgetting nothing and neglecting nothing.

"We see Thy handiwork in the vast panorama of nature's myriad beauties. We trace the divine artistry in all the glories and beauties displayed by the changing seasons. We see Thy divinity reflected in the law of evolution, which is constantly and ceaselessly at work.

"Most of all do we see Thee displayed in the spirit of man, which, rising to the highest heights of which it is capable, renders service in acts which exhibit its divine origin.

"Thou hast united Thyself with Thy children through all eternity. The tie that binds them to Thee is indissoluble; there is no event in life, or in what men call death, that can separate Thy children from Thee, or Thee from Thy children. By virtue of their heritage, they have a constant access to the divine fountain of all wisdom, all love, all inspiration and all knowledge.

"Our task is to teach them to equip themselves so that they

can play their part more fully in the great, infinite scheme of creation, so that they may become Thy instruments, spreading Thy purpose and disseminating the knowledge of Thy truth.

"Thus will they be enabled to succour the weak and sustain the needy; to help the fallen and give direction to those who have lost their way; to give food to the hungry and shelter to the homeless; to bring knowledge where ignorance reigns; to take light where all is darkness; so that the hundreds of thousands who do not know Thee may discover Thee and themselves and find their way to a life which could be rich in understanding did they but possess the key.

"Our task is to help to destroy the barriers between the two states of life, so that there may be a fullness of inspiration constantly descending through Thy instruments, that the influx of Thy love may be known and felt by all who need it, and that the tears of those who mourn may be dried by the knowledge of the spiritual laws which control all life.

"This is the prayer of Thy Indian servant who seeks to serve."

Chapter Four

'THE POWER OF LIFE'

WHEN Harry Edwards, the famous healer, visited Hannen Swaffer's home circle, he said, with typical modesty, to Silver Birch: "I am not concerned so much with what we can do but rather with the things we have been unable to do. How can we give greater service and become more in tune with those on your side?"

The spirit guide replied: "We are all co-operating in a great and mighty purpose whose object is to render the greatest possible service to the unfortunate ones, the weak, the suffering, the drifters, those whose heads are bowed with sorrow and whose hearts are filled with grief.

"The power of the spirit seeks to flood through instruments to bring its healing touch where it can find the opportunity, knowing that as instruments offer themselves for the fullest measure of co-operation, so there will come through them that force, that radiance, that will enable your world to realise what can be done when there is harmony.

"The power of the spirit is the power of life. The reason why there is life is because spirit is there. The power that fashioned the whole universe, majestic though it is and stupendously vast, is the same power which enables you to exist here and hereafter for all time. The power that enables you to love, to think, to care, to judge, to reflect, to decide, to weigh, to ponder, to be inspired, to reach the heights and depths of the whole gamut of human feelings, that power is the power of the spirit.

"The whole problem associated with every phase of mediumship is to regulate that flow of spirit power through instruments. As to how much and what kind of power can express itself depends entirely on the conditions that are available. It depends upon the qualities possessed by the human instrument and his willingness to develop along those lines which will make his co-operation greater and more effective. Always there is experimentation at work as new forces, new rays, new potencies are gradually introduced.

"All these are conditioned by the fitness, physical, mental and spiritual, of the instrument. If he provides a greater vehicle, then a greater part is manifest through him; if he provides a poorer vehicle, then a smaller amount of power is manifest through him.

"The point I wish to make is this, that many good people, religious people, think that the acme of spirit power was reached in days gone by, in the times described by the Bible, but that is not true. There has been progress made, and the spirit power that streams through some instruments today is far greater than has ever been known before on earth.

"My son, the best, the most that an old soul like myself can say is this: that for many years your earthly life has been guided to bring you to this culminating point. You are now achieving what was foreseen many years ago. This is the height of your attainment and you should rejoice in the fact that you are able to give the service that is available through your co-operation. Does that help?"

"Yes," said Edwards, "though it raises two points in my mind. The first is whether you can help us to make ourselves more fitting instruments. For example, here is a child with two deformed feet. One foot responds but not the other. Where lies the weakness? It must be the weakness with the instrument, because if one foot can be healed so can the other."

"It is not always possible to achieve the results that you would like to achieve or those who are working through you would like to achieve at the time," was Silver Birch's reply. "The greatest amount of good has to be done with the minimum amount of power. If the whole of the power is to be utilised for one case, then you would get spontaneous healing, but you would be exhausted for a long time to come.

"It is, as I tried to explain, experimental. Not even those who work with you can guarantee beforehand what will take place. They do not know the extent to which the results will be beneficial except to know that they will be beneficial. There are factors which are not known beforehand. There are conditions which impose restrictions on what can be done. It is a matter of great rejoicing that so much can be done where before it was not possible.

"That is the contribution that you have made through your willingness to go the whole way and say to those who use you: 'Here I am, take me. I trust you and I will follow.' Nothing would be more pleasurable than that every sufferer who presented himself for treatment should be instantaneously cured, and that all disease and deformity and sickness should fall away as if by magic. But that is not possible.

"There are problems. This is, comparatively, pioneering work. Those who are associated with you are busily engaged in knowing the reactions of each manifestation and bringing other elements to bear so as to improve the technique and the efficiency of what is done. I think I can say that you have observed the improvement that takes place on almost every occasion."

"Yes, that is so," agreed Edwards.

"The closer the co-operation, the more spirit power can be transmitted. There is also another great question involved and that concerns one of the limits. Here I realise that I tread on very controversial ground, but honesty compels me to express this viewpoint. One limit imposed, and always imposed, is what I would call the karmic debt of the patient, the relationship between mind and body determined by that individual's spiritual growth and attainment. Do I make myself clear?"

"I would like you to go further than that," Edwards quickly responded.

"I know you would," said Silver Birch. "This is very important and I want to say something that may surprise you. The important part of your work is not healing bodies but touching souls. Where you succeed in awakening the soul, in enabling it to have a greater mastery over the body, in enabling it to realise its true purpose and to begin to express itself in the fashion that it should, that is the greatest contribution that you can make.

"That is more important than healing the body, that is the eternal part of your labours. Every individual is a combination of mind, body and soul. There are interrelated factors; you cannot dismiss the influence of any one from the other.

"Disease is, in a large number of cases, primarily due to wrongful alignment of mind, body and spirit—that you know. And where you have perfect attunement between these triune aspects of man, and there is complete unity, there you have perfect health, stability, poise and awareness. But you do not meet that in your world except on very rare occasions.

"Every individual whom you see, who comes for treatment, is at a certain stage of growth. He has reached one particular rung in the ladder of his life, and that determines the amount of healing that can be transmitted to the individual. That is what I mean by the karmic debt.

"There are some whom you will be powerless to touch. The debt that has been incurred can be repaid only by discarding the physical body. There are others who have earned a second chance. You can bring them complete cures.

And there are others whose minds you are powerless to reach. You may improve their bodies for a time, but the condition will return in some other form."

Here the healer asked, "By that I assume that the karmic debt is superior to the healing forces that can be exercised?"

"Yes, I must insist on that," the guide told him, "because that is the individual's own contribution, his own life story, and there is no power to alter the natural law. You remember that I began by saying that all exists within the orbit or framework of natural law. Everything must operate with that provision. There are no miracles, as you know. There is no suspension or alteration or abrogation of natural law. It is all cause and effect. There is the limitation. It would be contrary to divine justice if any individual had the power to cancel the operation of cause and effect. What you can do is to free the soul, liberate the mind and then the body reaps the result."

"Is not that the way to help people to pay their karmic debts?" Edwards asked.

"That is so. That is why I say, if you succeed in touching the soul, and awakening it so that the individual is conscious of what he has to do, it is the important aspect of the work."

"We invariably find," commented Edwards, "there is a sense of inner joy, upliftment, higher expression, higher idealism, and that I take it is what you are saying."

"In the supreme moment of earth and heaven mingling and when, for a few fleeting moments, all barriers are gone, your own spirit finds itself," the guide told him. "It bursts its bonds and reaches that state of ecstasy which is the normal expression of the spirit."

Edwards returned to the question of karmic debt by asking, "I would like to make it quite clear that through healing it is possible so to touch the soul of individuals that you can help them to pay their karmic debts."

This brought from Silver Birch a declaration on the purpose of Spiritualism:

"The whole aim of this mission, of which your work and mine and all who are engaged in it are parts, is to awaken mankind, so that the largest possible number of individuals may be aware of themselves, to realise what they are, who they are, so that they can bring into being, as part of their normal, daily activity, all the qualities and attributes of the spirit.

"By so doing they will transform the whole of earthly life, changing it from a wilderness choked with the weeds of selfishness into a paradise filled with the flowers of idealism. That is what we are doing, or trying to do, with occasional success. Each soul who sees the light, who finds himself, who wakens out of the sleep, the materialistic sleep, is a soul who finds the road and begins to tread it with certainty and with knowledge."

Harry Edwards was moved by this passage to say: "I think you have given enough to help us. The actual healing is not of importance."

The wise old guide added: "I do not mean that we are indifferent to human suffering, that we do not care about the misery, pain and joylessness of those who are afflicted by the many diseases that are the result of wrongful living. But if we reach the causes of all these troubles, then we can end all this maladjustment between mind, body and spirit. Then we can fill the world with a radiance that it so much needs. Then the children of the Great Spirit will derive from earth that which they were intended to derive, the nobility, the grandeur, the richness, the dignity, the lustre and the beauty.

"And then, when death comes, they would pass through that door with ease, without pain, shedding the old body which had served its purpose for the next stage in their glorious existence . . .

"It is a joy to me to welcome any instrument. Those who labour to serve humanity are those I love. It is not always easy. No pathway of service can be easy, for if it was easy to serve the soul would not grow. That which is worth attaining is difficult. The prize to be earned is a prize that can be given not to the many but to the few.

"Strive to achieve your highest ideals—the secret dreams and prayers which are your great hopes and aspirations. Continue to be loyal to that light which you follow. Do not in any measure betray the trust that is reposed in you by those who love you. Hold aloft that torch of truth and let its radiance bring light to many who are in darkness.

"Continue so to order your own life that the power of the spirit may flow through you in increasing measure and magnitude, so that you may be the means of bringing blessings to those who are sorely afflicted and who know not where to turn.

"And rejoice that the Great Spirit has raised you up. It is still true, many are called, few are chosen. Continue to serve and know that as you serve so you will be served and love, divine and human, for it is the same thing, will continue to guide you and enable you to fulfil the purpose of your own earthly being."

Another psychic healer, who worked in the background, had for years cherished the ambition to sit with Silver Birch. He was invited to attend with his wife. After greeting them, the guide said:

"We are all workers with a common purpose. In one way or another, you, like myself and others from my world, are banded together to destroy the materialism which, alas, is far too rampant in your world. We are doing it quite successfully by showing how the application of the gifts of the spirit reveal a truer understanding of life's meanings, its purpose, of human destiny, of the relationship between you and the Great

Spirit and between all the children of the Great Spirit wherever they may dwell.

"Whatever form the gifts of the spirit take, when they are exercised, they are a revelation that materialism is founded on a falsity, for you, like I, are helping to demonstrate the fundamental, eternal truth that man is a spiritual being, that he is like the Great Spirit in tiny miniature, but possessing, albeit in latent form, all that pertains to divinity. If by laying hands on one who is sick, one who has despair because no relief has been obtainable elsewhere, you show that the power of the spirit brings healing in its train, then not only do you heal the body but you touch a soul. That is part of my mission, to touch souls, to awaken them from their long sleep so that they may have a realisation of what they really are."

Then the guide dealt with a problem raised by the healer, who described his reactions while giving treatment.

"We are always pleased to learn what happens when the power of the spirit streams through instruments," said Silver Birch. "The flood of spirit power is very largely a matter of experiment. It is not all planned beforehand, except in the broad outlines. The amount of any power, force, ray, or vibration that can be transmitted through any medium, is dependent upon the circumstances that prevail at the time. The medium's health, for instance, is one factor. The medium's mood is another factor, whether it is equable or anxious. The whole question of the receptivity of the medium is also naturally involved.

"In addition to that there are the other circumstances concerned with the people around the medium. If it is a circle, then the individual members of it all contribute something. Much has to be taken into account. Then there is the patient, the sufferer, the one who is to be healed, his or her circumstances, spiritual, mental and physical.

All of these will affect the amount of spirit power that can be transmitted.

"Now it is idle to pretend, for a single moment, that transmitting spirit power through a medium and its return has no effect on the instrument through whom it comes. You are not using a conduit; you are using a human organism with a spirit, with a mind, with a most complex arrangement of bodily functions and you cannot send through that a stream of life-giving, dynamic power without some reaction.

"All depends on how well developed the instrument is. That is why, so often, it is urged, again and again, that the would-be medium, the potential healer, should nurture his gift under the wise guardianship of an experienced person plus, and this of course is the most important, the co-operation of the spirit guide who is to work through that individual. It is only after a long, long process of training that the gift can be so unfolded that the right amount of spirit power can be transmitted in the best form where it can produce the most successful results.

"You have to have the desire to develop the gift. You have to regulate your own life so that cleanliness and right thinking will be the dominant motives. You have to be sure that the physical body, the temple of the spirit, is as pure as you can make it. You have to keep a watchful eye on your own exertions so that you do not jeopardise your own health. You have to rest occasionally so that in these periods of recuperation the necessary adjustments can be made. Now where there are instruments who are prepared to give the necessary co-operation, there you will find the best results.

"You must be affected by the healing that you do because you are a spiritual being, and whatever comes through you leaves its mark on you, particularly mentally and physically. And if it is a very drastic case, one in which an added call is made upon your resources, which means that additional power has to come through, you must expect a reaction, temporary though it will be, until adjustment is made."

When the healer tried to express his thanks Silver Birch said: "Thank the Great Spirit, for it is the Great Spirit we are trying to serve. We are only ministers and we do not require that any praise, or glory, or prayers, or appreciation should be given to us. Let us always recognise that we are all the instruments of a great purpose, each of us striving to do our part so as to make it easier, better and happier for others."

Then the visitor said that he had heard many people talk of healing "miracles" but he had never seen these cases. His own healing worked on different lines. "Do you think that different people are gifted with a different kind of healing?" he asked.

"There are many diversities, but it is the same spirit," answered the guide. "The power of the spirit is infinite and, being infinite, it has an infinite number of variations. No individuals are exactly alike, not even twins, though they bear the closest possible resemblance. Thus it is that because of infinite variations the power of the spirit is unable to express itself in a similar way through different mediums. It is all governed by the circumstances that rule, for everything in the whole universe, whether it be large or small, is regulated by a natural law.

"Those who attend here regularly and who have listened for many years know that this is a theme on which I harp constantly. It is the theme of the constancy of the natural law. I know nothing of a jealous, vengeful deity, a capricious or partisan God. I have seen the operation of natural laws in every aspect of universal life, not only in your world of matter, but in the world of spirit which is my natural habitat, and wherever I have gone I find that natural law rules.

"There is no chance, no caprice, no miracle, no accident.

All is due to cause and effect which follow one another in a sequence that is methodically exact and inviolable. Natural law rules throughout the whole universe and all that takes place, no matter where you look, whether it be in the realm of insect life, in human life, or in planetary life, always you will see that law is in operation.

"These laws take no cognisance of human desire or will. Your ideas, your views, your wishes will not change the natural law. The law has always been in operation: it is in operation now, it will continue to operate, for time is eternal and the law is eternal, too. I know nothing of miracles. I do know that the power of the spirit, working according to natural law, though it may be a law not yet revealed or understood by those on earth, is capable of working seeming miracles.

"The power of the spirit is life. Where there is life there is spirit, where there is spirit there is life. Where the power of the spirit can be transmitted in a sufficiently full measure it can bring in its train all the properties of life and thus you have what many regard as miracles.

"They take place because another law is brought into operation. You see the effect of some cause, the cripple is made whole, the deaf begin to hear, the blind to see. The same power which enabled that person in the first place to live and move and walk and breathe and think and see and hear, the same power is in operation again and producing similar results. You, because you are a spirit, animate a physical frame which apart from your spirit has no life of its own. Withdraw the spirit and you have what is called death, inertia: the instrument has no vitalising power streaming through it. Now if you can bring the power of the spirit to work in parts of that body which are diseased you can make the life-giving force reproduce what has been lost."

'To strip away all falsities'

"Oh Great White Spirit, we seek, as always, to interpret Thee as Thou truly art. We desire to strip away all the falsities, the shams and misrepresentations which for too long have prevented Thy children from gaining a clear conception of Thee.

"In order to understand themselves they must appreciate the power which is behind all life and to realise their relationship to it.

"Thou art not a deified man with human passions and weaknesses. Thou art not a tribal god. Thou art not Jehovah. Thou art not a deity with favours to offer to selected members of Thy family.

"Thou art the Great Spirit, the first primal cause, the supreme arbiter of all destiny, the king of all kings, the epitome of perfect love and wisdom. Thou art the power which fashioned the whole wondrous universe and has set in motion all the laws which regulate every phase of its activity.

"Thou art the mind which has planned and directed all things. Thine is the spirit which broods over all and has given life to man so that he can become like Thee and grow and evolve towards perfection.

"We seek to reveal Thee and Thy laws so that mankind can obtain a true and comprehensive picture of his place in the divine scheme and know the part that he must play to fulfil his destiny.

"Thou hast raised him up from the brutish beasts of the field. Thou hast filled him with Thine own divinity, spirit of Thy spirit, so that he can share with Thee in helping to shape the whole plan of life.

"He is intended to fulfil that heritage, to exercise that spirit within him, and in so doing fill the world with beauty, loveliness, grace and splendour, and enable all the riches and wealth of the spirit and the mind to be enjoyed alike by all Thy children.

"There need not be darkness or cruelty, greed, cunning or avarice. All these are excrescences which can be swept away if Thy children would but call into activity the power with which Thou hast endowed them.

"It is to teach them how to realise all these powers that we labour, so that they may enjoy on earth that kingdom which could be theirs and truly prepare themselves for the richer kingdom which is their inevitable destiny beyond the grave.

"That is the prayer of Thy Indian Servant who seeks to serve."

Chapter Five

'TO DWELL IN LIBERTY'

ARE spirit guides more spiritually advanced than their medium charges? Is there any point in psychic research? Can God be described as almighty and merciful? These were just a few of the subjects raised when Silver Birch answered questions submitted by readers of "Psychic News." Of course, one of the many wonders about Silver Birch was that never was he unable to answer satisfactorily a point put to him. Incidentally, the medium was not told in advance what the questions were to be.

So it was that when the guide was asked, "What is the greatest contribution Spiritualism has to make to the modern world?" he replied: "The greatest contribution that this knowledge has is to bring freedom in all its diverse ramifications to the children of the Great Spirit. It frees them from all the bondage to which they have been subject. It removes them from the prison-house of ignorance by showing them that the door of knowledge has opened wide for them. It enables them to live in the sunlight instead of in the shadow.

"It frees them from all the tyranny of superstition and priestcraft. It teaches them to be doughty warriors in the fight for truth everywhere. It makes them conscious of the divinity within them. It enables them to recognise the mutual tie of the spirit that exists in every other child of the Great Spirit.

"It shows them how they can help to build a new world where there is no hatred, no difference of colour or race, where the only superiors are those who have earned it by their greater service. It enriches their knowledge; it equips their mind; it fortifies their spirit and teaches them how to live so that they are worthy of their divine birthright. That is the great contribution this knowledge makes.

"Man was born to be free, to dwell in liberty; he was not born to be a slave, bound and fettered. His life should be full of richness, the richness of mind and body and spirit. All knowledge should be open to him, all truth, all wisdom, all inspiration. He should dwell in the splendour of the spirit with none of the cramping, irksome, vexatious restrictions imposed upon him by those who would deny his heritage and thwart his destiny."

The next question was, "Is it better that Spiritualism should grow as it is growing, as an influence, rather than as a formally organised faith?"

"I would deny that it is a faith," said Silver Birch, "it is a knowledge. You cannot control the breath of the wind; you cannot control the growth or the spread of knowledge. Truth will blossom of her own accord. You cannot regulate it. You can only provide the means by which it becomes accessible to more and more people. What the effect of this knowledge will be you cannot estimate before; you cannot lay down any rules or control the channels of its dissemination.

"All you can do is to be faithful to your own responsibility, to discharge your duty in the light of your understanding, to help where you can, to pass on what you have received, and let the balm of the spirit take its own course. It is a leaven. It will continue to infiltrate and permeate throughout all branches of human activity. Each must do what he thinks is best and spread knowledge according to the way he thinks it will be of service."

Another question was, "Would you say that guides are always spiritually in advance of their mediums?"

"No, I would not," answered Silver Birch. "It depends upon the task that has to be performed and it also depends upon the construction that you give to the word 'guide.' Those in our world who are associated with earthly instruments work in co-operation. There is usually a band attached to each medium, and there is at the head the directing intelligence.

"He is the one who should be more properly described as the guide, for the rest are working under his direction and although, occasionally, some of them may speak through the medium, they do so only at the request of the one in charge. But their functioning is not quite the same. That is why you sometimes use the word 'control' to mark the difference between two kinds of beings who manifest through mediums.

"If you refer to the usual method that is employed in the case of trance mediums, then it is always true that the guide in charge is the spiritual superior of the medium. But in certain physical phenomena, many of those employed in the group to accomplish results need not be of great spiritual attainment. In fact, some of them can best fulfil their function because of their proximity to earthly conditions, and in such cases it is true to say that the members of the spirit band are not necessarily more spiritually advanced than the medium that is used. But it is true in the general sense of the guide that is the controlling, directing influence and the medium, otherwise the initiative could not very well come from our side."

The next question was, "Is a medium's health affected by trance mediumship?"

"It should not be affected in any way except for the better," said the guide, "if he is used according to the known laws that regulate trance mediumship. Obviously, if a trance medium were to allow the situation to get out of hand by indulging in too many sittings, for example, three or four each day, then it might have some adverse effect upon the health. But if the sittings follow the normal course, if there are one or two over stated periods and the instrument has been wisely developed, then the results must be an increase in the health of the medium, because the power of the spirit constantly streaming through earthly instruments is one that is so vitalising that it leaves a regenerative effect. Wisely used, all mediumship will improve the health; unwisely used, it will act as a deterrent."

"That is a very interesting question," said Silver Birch when asked, "Is there any truth in the doctrine that thought possesses real tangible power?"

"Thought has potency; let there be no mistake about that, because thought is one of the creative processes of life. Thought is a reality on its own plane of expression, but it is limited according to the sphere in which it is used.

"You are dwelling in an earthly world where you register through five material senses, and you have reached only that stage of development where you are capable of expressing yourself in this materialistic fashion. You have not yet evolved to the stage where all people can communicate by the power of telepathy. That is something which is still to be attained. In your present development you are spiritual beings compelled to use material means for your expression. That places a restriction and limitation on the power of thought, because it is only when that thought takes material form that you are able to become aware of it.

"Thought is real on its own plane of expression, but it is unknown to you, as you are at present, until it is clothed with matter. In our world, where we do not have the thraldom of the flesh, thought has a far greater reality, for we are living in a world of thought—the basis of our reality is the expression of the spirit or the mind, or the soul, and thought is one of its fundamental expressions.

"You must not encourage people to think that whilst they are on earth thought can ever be a substitute for work, labour or activity. It is a useful auxiliary, but not a substitute. You must accomplish your results by the work that you can do. You cannot abolish physical activity and say all that is necessary will be accomplished by the power of thought. You must place it in its proper perspective."

"Used as a motive for physical activity in this world?" asked a circle member.

"Yes, and it has an unconscious use," continued Silver Birch, "because in your limited development you are unable to harness its potency."

"But you can harness our thoughts into a potency if you wish to do so," commented the same sitter.

"Yes, because we are working through your minds and through your spirits," said the guide, "but what I am most anxious to do is to discourage the idea that your problems can be solved by mass concentrations of thought. However useful or helpful thought may be, it is no substitute for the work that you must do. That may be an unpopular doctrine to preach, but it is the truth as I see it."

Another member of the circle said: "If all the prayers that were offered before the war could not prevent the war—surely that is the answer. And they came from all over Europe, Germany as well."

"I would agree with that," remarked Silver Birch. "Thought has its limitation in a material world where matter is the basis of recognition. It must be so, but, on the other hand, I do not wish to dismiss the value of thought, or the place that it has in the scheme of life."

"It can help those expressing the good thought, apart from the effect elsewhere," was another sitter's comment. And someone else added, "If we all wish well of America, it is reacting well on us."

"And in the healing of absent people," said Silver Birch, "thought is one of the means for obtaining cures. But then you must remember that it is regulated by the agency of the spirit. So few people in your world understand how to deal with the mental equipment of the individual. That, incidentally, is part of the next stage of human evolution. Thought should be a useful precursor to action. Your action should be the result of well-regulated thought. But how many are there who know how to use the power of thought? How many are there who could sit, even for five minutes, with their minds concentrated only on one thought? Very, very few."

The guide was next asked, "With regard to absent healing, does it help if the patient co-operates at the time of the healing?"

"I would say," began the answer, again without hesitation, "that in most cases it is a help because it aids the process of attunement. That may cause controversy, but that is my view. It is easier as a rule to obtain results when you have knowledge rather than ignorance. When you have completed the spiritual circuit by having the one attuned, the instrument through whom the healing force has to radiate, and, at the other end, the one who is to receive it, attuned to the same pitch, then it is easier for the result to be obtained.

"I know it is being claimed that in many cases excellent results are obtained when the sick man or woman is unaware of what is happening, but that is due to the fact that very often the results are achieved in his or her sleep state when there is more accessibility to the spirit body."

"Are you in favour of psychical research?" the guide was asked. He replied:

"The trouble in attempting to answer these questions is to obtain an agreement on the terms which are being used, as to the meaning that you attach to them. There is a certain meaning attached to the term 'psychical research' which amongst those who call themselves Spiritualists is not one of great liking. All these sittings, or seances, or gatherings, are research in its real meaning, for constantly we are examining the means by which the power of the spirit is able to have a greater manifestation in your world.

"You are learning from us; we are learning from you. I am in favour of all the research where the motive is to desire knowledge and when that knowledge is attained to use it for the good of all mankind. I am not in favour of blind-alley research whose motive is to try to cast doubts about phenomena obtained through mediums. If the motive is sincere, then it is research; if it is insincere, then it is not research. Real research has our approval."

"What is the answer to the clerical jibe that Spiritualism has nothing new to contribute to the world?"

"I do not think it is a jibe," was the spirit reply. "We have nothing new to contribute to the world except one thing, that for the first time in human history we place religion upon the foundation of demonstration, that we remove it out of the realm of faith, hope and speculation and say here is that which can be proved. Apart from that there is nothing new, but I don't know that the Nazarene taught anything that was new. Surely the test is not newness or novelty, but is it true?"

After a tribute had been paid to the remarkable intelligence of his replies, Silver Birch explained: "We have access to organised knowledge in a form which is unknown in your world, whereas you are dependent upon the residue of knowledge collected by individuals. We have all that information available to us—to those who know how to obtain it instantly.

"One of the marvels of life in our world is the supreme and superb organisation, for not only is it true in the realm of knowledge, it is equally as true in all the riches of the spirit, in literature, in art, in music. All that has ever been known is instantly available to us, and much that is still unknown to you is at our disposal."

It was at another meeting of the circle that Silver Birch was asked, "Is it right to term the Great Spirit almighty and merciful?"

"I see nothing to quarrel with in the use of those two descriptions," he replied. "The Great Spirit is almighty because all power is vested in the natural laws that control the universe and all the life in all the forms that exist in the universe. There is nothing higher, greater, more powerful than the Great Spirit. The governance of the universe is directed by law, unfailing wisdom, a beneficent purpose, for always all forms of life are evolving from the darkness towards the light, from the lower towards the higher, from imperfection towards perfection.

"That shows that the quality of mercy is part of the divine purpose. But what must always be included is the mechanical nature of these laws—mechanical in the sense that they are so perfect that none has the power to interfere with the sequence of cause and effect.

"There is no one, however exalted spiritually he may be, who can prevent effect following cause with mathematical certainty. That is the mechanical aspect. I use the word because it is difficult to find words, and yet the word 'mechanical' suggests the machine without the dynamic, driving, intelligent, conscious, purposive force behind it.

"The conception that I would like to see fostered is the one of the Great Spirit, almighty, merciful, perfect, infinite, but at the same time get rid of the idea of personality in the human sense in which it is understood on earth. But you must remember that an infinite spirit has many manifestations. You, yourself, are the Great Spirit in miniature. You contain within yourselves the spark of perfection that is the spirit, the spirit which is the essence of all life. Without that divine spark you cannot exist. Yet you, as you are manifest in an earthly personality, are not perfect.

"The spark of spirit is perfection, the aspect of consciousness revealed through your physical body is very imperfect. After death you will manifest in the etheric, the astral, the spiritual body—it does not matter which term you use, so long as you understand what you mean by it. You will then be less imperfect than you are now. As you evolve in the realms of spirit, you will express less and less imperfection, and more and more of the latent divinity will rise to the surface. So that whilst you are both imperfect and perfect, it is but a question of degree."

A sitter commented, "Very much as a rosebud is not a perfect rose, but becomes so when it is fully developed."

"To some degree," replied the guide, "but it is complicated by the fact that perfection is an infinite process. You cannot achieve perfection; there is no finality to knowledge, wisdom, understanding or truth, because as the mind and the spirit grow their capacity becomes increased, and what is unattainable now will be attainable in the years to come. As you climb and reach out to the rung that was beyond your reach yesterday, today you realise that another rung has come within your horizon. It is an infinite process. You do not achieve perfection. If you could achieve it, then evolution would be meaningless."

Commenting on questions put by members of the circle, Silver Birch said: "You are trying, and you should persevere, to gain a conception of something that is beyond finite language, that can be glimpsed and perhaps comprehended, even when it cannot be expressed. You must have sometimes come across a scene of such ineffable beauty that you have felt there are no words and no language and no artist capable of expressing it, yet you feel it, and you know it. Now it is just like that. You are trying to put into finite language infinite terms."

"I suppose," said a sitter, "a rough and ready definition of the Great Spirit would be the aggregate of all spiritual consciousness in the world."

"Yes," replied the guide, "except that consciousness has many manifestations, and there is no phase of being or activity that is outside the orbit of the Great Spirit, because the laws, the natural laws, automatically include everything in the universe.

"There is no phase of motion, vibration, animal life, bird life, plant life, insect life, vegetable life, floral life, marine life, human life, spiritual life, that is not regulated by law. The universe is not discordant; it is one harmony on a grand scale. Once you perceive the key, the key that enables you to understand, it is very simple—that is, the universal law controls all, and that law is the result of the Great Spirit. The law is the Great Spirit, the Great Spirit is the law.

"It is impersonal in the sense that it is not in any way a magnification of human beings, but it is personal in the sense that it is embraced within all forms of spiritual, mental and physical activity. By that I want it made clear that you, as human beings, are within the framework of the Great Spirit, and have an access to it because you contribute a vital part to it."

A member of the circle asked, "Arising from what you said, are the laws of the Great Spirit fixed, or are they still being made?"

"The laws have always been in existence," said Silver Birch, "because being perfect there is no action that can take place outside their orbit. All has been provided, for the law has taken cognisance. If fresh laws had to be made, then the Great Spirit would cease to be perfect, for it would mean that a need has arisen which was not foreseen."

"So," said the same questioner, "the laws of the Great Spirit are the blueprint of perfection and we all are slowly trying to pattern ourselves to the blueprint of perfection."

"That is a very good approximation," responded the guide. "Here you all are, evolving beings in an evolving world that is part of a tremendous universe in which every aspect is subject to laws which provide for every circumstance that can arise.

"You cannot go outside the laws. Your life, your being, your activity is circumscribed by those laws. It is for you to discover how to harmonise your thought, your word, your deed, the whole of your life so that it is in unity with these laws. Then you will have got rid of disease, poverty and all the chaotic conditions which belong to the darkness of ignorance. That is why, whenever I am questioned about free will, I always have to say that it is not an unfettered free will, it is part of a free will circumscribed by natural law."

When Silver Birch was asked to express his opinion about the Ten Commandments—it was even suggested that he should form another set—the guide agreed they were out of date.

"You must not regard the power of the spirit as it was expressed in any period in man's long history as being the final word in all divine revelation," he said. "Your world must realise that revelation is continuous and progressive, fitting itself to the stage of understanding of the people to whom it comes.

"It must not be so far ahead of them that they cannot understand it. It must only be so much in front that it is within their grasp. Always the wisdom of the power of the spirit is but one step ahead, and when man achieves that step, he is ready for the next in the infinite ladder of wisdom.

"Why should that which obtained in the days when the race was still in its comparative infancy and had special application to people governed by special conditions be made to fit circumstances of today which are vastly different? But I only have one commandment, that you serve one another, that is all."

The guide's answer led to a discussion during which Silver Birch said:

"Sometimes I wish I could endow you all with the vision of the spirit, so that you could see the intricate organisation that does exist in our world, and the care, the almost supreme care, with which plans are made and influences exerted in all the countries of your world. All the foresight born of long years of wisdom is used, and even then it sometimes miscarries. We too have our failures as well as our successes.

"But, speaking for myself, I can only say that I have been very richly blessed because I have earned so much love and so much respect. My task has been made far easier than many others who have, despite strenuous exertion, failed to accomplish their mission. Look on the road we have travelled, from complete obscurity to now what is virtually a mission which has penetrated the far corners of the earth. And it is not yet ended.

"We are at the moment confronted with conditions of great difficulty, but, despite them all, we are still able to pour a little light into a greatly darkened world."

"How can awareness of the Great Spirit be achieved?" was another question addressed to the guide.

"First they must have clearly in their minds what they mean by the Great Spirit of life. Their conceptions of the Great Spirit have for too long been based on false notions.

"Inevitably the Great Spirit cannot be expressed in finite terms. Infinity cannot be expressed in finite language, and so always the Great Spirit must elude and be beyond the complete understanding of minds which are restricted on earth.

"But, because you are spiritual beings, because the divine spark is within you, because in degree you possess qualities of the Great Spirit, you can become aware of all that vital, dynamic, supreme power which is responsible for every phase of life. But this awareness is a matter of degree.

"You must learn to still the physical senses. You must learn how to be impervious to the clangour, to the noisy discord, to the clash of your material world. You must learn how to be at peace within; how to harness your soul to the great primal forces which are ever round and about you. You must learn the secret of tranquillity that comes from within when the soul finds itself and knows that it is at one with the power behind life.

"That requires time and patience and knowledge. But as you equip yourself to register subtle, delicate vibrations of the spiritual life, which always teems about your being, you will become aware of the marvellous potentialities of your own innate spirit, and you will become aware of the Great Spirit within you. But it is not easy."

On another occasion Silver Birch was asked to elaborate on "The power of the Spirit," a phrase he frequently used. Was it tangible? Could it be described? Without a moment's pause, the guide answered thus:

"You use words that are difficult to interpret. When you say 'tangible' what do you mean? Do you mean does it conform to any perception by the five senses? No, it does not.

"Is it real? Yes, it is as real as knowledge, as real as wisdom, as real as evolution, as real as friendship, as real as love, as real as any invisible force that exists. It is tangible on our plane of expression but imperceptible except to those who are sensitive and can appreciate its reality.

"It is a power, a divine power, a power which operates in many lives. Those who are ignorant, those who are prejudiced, those who allow their lives to be ordered by superstition, provide mental barriers, each of which is an obstacle to the power of the spirit, and the nature of the obstacle determines the time that it will take to break it down.

"There are some people who go through the whole of earthly life without having any inkling of the truth. They are unaware that life is spirit, that spirit is life, that the whole of your world depends for its maintenance upon the power of the spirit.

"These people are blind, deaf and dumb to the realities of spirit, and they live in this material prison until death releases them. And even then, as you know, there is a long process of adjustment before they are able to appreciate reality.

"Others receive occasional glimpses and in these fleeting moments are aware of that higher, transcendental power which shapes and governs and guides all the processes of life.

"And then there are those who, like yourselves, have received direct knowledge and are accessible to the power of the spirit day by day. You have opened your hearts, your minds, your souls and you are ready to become instruments of that same power which sustains the whole of life and which now seeks to be used through you so that others can be touched and quickened by it.

"It is all part of one power. The power that regulates all the processes of life is part of that power which we use and is used here to enable me to speak."

In answer to another question Silver Birch said: "Have faith, not blind faith, but faith founded on knowledge. Have confidence. It is the old, old cry. It is nothing new I have to tell you, but I do reiterate it with all the eloquence at my command so that it shall become part of the very fabric of your being. Have confidence.

"You do your part, we will do ours. We shall not fail you. There is a vast range of inspiration that you can have access to if you so desire, but fear, doubt, uncertainty, these are discords that interfere and should have no place in your consciousness.

"There is a lot of work to be done. I want you to help me by your faithful constancy of purpose. There are many obstacles that even I, with all my long experience, find difficult to conquer. You must help me by being faithful and confident and, above all, fearless, by not allowing any thought of fear, no worry or anxiety to take root in your beings.

"Problems will cross your path, but you will cross them: they will not stay. There will be no difficulty so great that you cannot solve it, no load so heavy that you cannot bear it upon your shoulders. Have no fear. Face whatever the morrow brings you with resolute heart and a determined spirit and all will be well.

"There are many thousands who will seek your aid and you must be ready to help them and thus fulfil the purpose of your own existence, for when all is said and done, unless you serve, unless you give to others that which you have received, you are not living in your lives the implications of the knowledge that has been vouchsafed to you.

"There is much to be done. Let us with joyful anticipation take up our task knowing that here and there will be souls who will rejoice because of what we have done.

"And always to the Great Spirit we turn, for Thine is the power which enables us all to live, Thine is the power which uplifts, Thine is the power which heals, Thine is the power which illumines. We strive to express it in all its rich measure so that those who know it not may realise the wondrous divinity which is at their disposal. The Great Spirit bless you all."

At yet another sitting, more questions were put to the spirit sage. In fact, over the years he answered countless hundreds. These were submitted by admirers the world over. "We know where the spirit goes to," wrote one, "but where does it come from?"

"Does he know where it goes?" asked Silver Birch. "Where does it go?"

"I take it," said the member of the circle who put the questions, "that he means it passes on to the next world, where you are."

"But," said Silver Birch, "your world uses such loose terms like 'next world.' All life is one life with infinite gradations. You are as much now in the next world as ever you will be. It is only a question of the rate of your vibration.

"You are as much a spiritual being now as ever you will be—death will not transform you into a spiritual being, death will not enhance your spiritual stature by one iota.

"You are spirit, you always were spirit, you always will be spirit, and at present you are aware of that portion of spirit which is manifested in a physical body.

"As you evolve after what is called death, more and more of the unexpressed spirit will be able to display itself, but spirit has never gone anywhere, it has never come from anywhere. It always was, it always is, it always will be."

"How," asked a member of the circle, "did it express itself before it found earth expression? I suppose that is what he means."

"Spirit always exists as spirit," was the reply, "but it does not exist as individual or individuated spirit until it has an embodiment in matter. Individuality comes to spirit from its association with an earthly body.

"Just as the individuality of a domestic animal depends on its association with man, I suppose?" said this sitter, and the guide's reply was: "Yes."

"When we lose this physical body," said another sitter, "shall not we still be individuals?"

"More so," was the answer.

"But gradually you merge into what you call the Great Spirit, because you are more a part of it," was an opinion put by a member of the circle.

"You are still an individual," explained Silver Birch, "because you yourself are expressing latent qualities which depend for their expression on your evolution.

"The more you evolve, the more of the unexpressed self comes to the surface. That means more of perfection is being expressed, and because more of perfection is being expressed the closer you are to the Great Spirit.

"If perfection were a finite process, then you would, in a

stated time, merge with the Great Spirit, but it is an infinite process, for the more you evolve the more you realise there is to be evolved, so that you are becoming more and more individualised as time goes on."

The next question was: "Are those who have passed on conscious of the thoughts and prayers we send up to them, and are they able to use the power of the love sent to them in their work?"

"It depends," was the reply, "on the people concerned as to whether there is a kinship of love or affection between them, but very largely it is true that all sincere thought and prayer, all desire to be of any service gives it the wing of direction towards the one to whom it is expressed and does help them."

Yet another question was, "Will there always be another chance for everybody?"

"Of course, there is," said Silver Birch.

"If there were not a second chance, then the universe would not be ruled by divine love and justice.

"If the story of man ended with the earthly grave, then the world would be full of mistakes, full of people who have never had compensation or even retribution for the life they have lived.

"The great glory of the knowledge we strive to bring to your world is that life does not end with death, that all who have suffered, that all who have failed, are provided with an opportunity of self-redemption, that the tears of frustration are wiped away in the knowledge of what can be achieved, that all who have desired to enrich their world and failed can add their lustre to mankind's growth.

"Life goes on, and in doing so it provides everybody with another chance to express their innate gifts, the gifts that were denied a manifestation on earth; and conversely it provides the means of remedial discipline for those who have foolishly strutted and imagined that they had been able to escape the natural laws that ruled over all.

"There is no greater justice than divine justice. None cheats it, none thwarts it, all come within the realm of its ordinance. In that knowledge, the kindly and the decent have nothing to fear; it is only those who have been selfish who need be afraid."

When the conversation turned to the men who are being killed in war, the guide said:

"Do not judge eternity by the infinitesimal fragment of earthly life. Do not judge the universe by your world. Life does not end with death.

"The word 'finis' does not appear on the book of life because the body has come to its end. Life goes on and its story is continued and developed amidst scenes of greater splendour, beauty and richness than those who dwell on earth have any conception.

"It is sad that fruit should drop from the tree before it is ripe, but there are compensations. Love and life are eternal, and those who leave the physical body in time of war before their spirits have had an opportunity for maturity are able to complete their unfoldment elsewhere."

Yet another question was, "How does an avowed materialist fare when he passes over?" Silver Birch said:

"Your world for too long has been deluded with the idea that the ones who call themselves religious possess a spiritual advantage over their fellows. That is not axiomatic. You are not the spiritual superior of your fellow because you believe in certain theological doctrines.

"The only test which is applied is the test of daily life. Your spiritual nature is exactly what you have made it to be, and there are many materialists and atheists and rationalists and agnostics who are the spiritual superiors of thousands who think that they are amongst the elect because they have bowed the knee in homage to the Great Spirit and accept certain doctrines.

"The test is not what you believe, but what you have done, otherwise there would be a complete mockery of divine justice."

Then someone said: "We are told we must fight vested interests. How can we do this?" The guide replied: "By fighting them. If he sees iniquity, let him wage war on it.

"He need not think that it falls to each man to fight the supreme tyrant of your earthly world. There is a vested interest in every little village, in every city, in every town—let him declare war on that.

"It is unfortunately true that mankind's eyes are so holden that he sees so little of the truth that he desires to rescue others when he is not rescued himself.

"He who wishes to reform the world should begin by reforming himself. Our task is to state simply eternal truths. Once you understand them then you have to spread them and in spreading them you have to clear out of the way all the impediments and obstacles and all whose desire is to maintain the old because it gives them a vested interest.

"That is what I mean. You have to fight all the selfish principles, you have to fight all the tyrants, large or small; all those who live upon the backs of the people, all the parasitical growths of those who make a profit out of disease and slums, all those who enrich themselves at the expense of their fellows.

"Surely there is no need for a detailed campaign to be outlined. Any who possess grains of sense can see where the task lies."

"The writer wants you to recommend a political party," it was stated.

"I don't care what party they join," said the guide. "I am only concerned with the life that is lived. I realise that as long as you keep to simple truths you cannot go wrong."

Then as the circle was not to sit for some time the guide said:

"I would like to tell you that, as always, the parting is not a real one. I shall be with you all the time.

"Together we have been enabled to give some service and to reach souls who but for our little help might still be wandering in the mists of difficulties, doubts and despair.

"Let us rejoice that we can count a number who have been aided by our ministrations, who turn their faces, radiant with new-born knowledge, towards us, and are grateful for our combined labours and exertions.

"Always our task is directed towards the service of humanity, to those who need the help that we can give them.

"We are destroying ignorance, we are ridding your world of prejudice and superstition. The foes that belong to the darkness gradually retreat as the light of knowledge sweeps them by, and always the spirit of man is on the march onwards to the uplands of truth and wisdom.

"Our task is to help that onward march, to teach all how to find liberation and freedom, how to deliver themselves from the bondage which has afflicted them for too long.

"There are far too many living in prisons when the doors are wide open, and they can enjoy all the fruits of liberation.

"That is our supreme task—to raise up man, to make him aware of the infinite power within him that he might live a life of fullness and service, that he might enjoy the nobility and dignity that should be his, that he might live in full freedom, fearing none, desiring only to add to the world's lustre by the unfoldment and quickening of his own spiritual gifts.

"Picture your world as it could be; note the differences that you have made throughout all the darkness of medieval superstition, and realise that you are on the threshold even now of new and vast spiritual adventures.

"There is a tremendous territory of knowledge awaiting

your exploration, and we ask you to help us in the task of teaching all how to share the richness that awaits them, how to equip themselves for this task, how to live that they may be worthy of their heritage and acquit themselves of their divine kinship.

"The voice of the spirit will be still for a while, but the power of the spirit will continue."

'To quicken the spirit'

"Oh, Great White Spirit, Thine is the infinite intelligence which has conceived the mighty universe. Thine are the laws which control and regulate the ceaseless panorama of daily events. Thine is the power which sustains all that is contained within it. Thine is the spirit which has given life to forms of matter and raised man up out of the animal kingdom into the divine awareness which he now possesses.

"We represent Thee as the supreme law, unchangeable, unalterable, immutable, omnipotent, for naught happens outside the confines of Thy law. Every phase of being throughout the whole world pays silent tribute to the inflexibility of its working. We who have had the larger experience in Thy spiritual domain, add our meed of praise to the perfection with which the whole of life is directed and governed by that power which some call God and we the Great Spirit.

"It is a knowledge of Thy law in all its ramifications that we seek to spread so that understanding it Thy children everywhere may reap that fullness of life and enjoy all that Thou hast so plentifully provided, and also fashion those systems which will enable the world of matter to live in peace.

"We seek to drive out all the fear that belongs to the darkness of men's ignorance, to make them understand the true place of death in the scheme of life, to awaken them to their own potentialities, that they may realise the infinite spirit that exists within their own natures. We strive to teach them of this so that they may know of the tie of spiritual kinship that exists between them and Thee and between all Thy children everywhere.

"Thy spirit girdles the whole world. The thread of Thy divinity runs through every being, and all who live, no matter who they are, what they are, or where they are, for ever bound to Thee by an enduring divine relationship that can never be destroyed.

"There is no necessity for any man to stand between Thy children and Thee. Because of their natural heritage they have complete access to all the infinite storehouses of wisdom, love, knowledge and truth that Thou hast provided.

"Our task is to quicken the spirit within man, so that finding full expression all Thy children will live lives that Thou intended should be their portion. Thus will they fulfil their destiny in the world in which they live. Thus will they discharge all their divine obligations. Thus will they render that service enabling a broken world to be healed and love and goodwill to reign among Thy children everywhere. Thus will they live in the light of understanding, having for ever turned their backs on the darkness which prevented them from seeing Thee in all Thy full radiance.

"This is the prayer of Thy Indian servant, who seeks to serve."

Chapter Six

'THERE IS NO FINALITY'

THESE days, due to modern technology, news can boomerang across the world in seconds. So it is that an event which may have happened thousands of miles away can rapidly be seen on television, reported on the radio or featured in newspapers. Truth to tell so much of what we see, hear and read is bad news. Almost daily acts of violence and human misery flit across our TV screens.

Yet humanity, Silver Birch insisted, was progressing. He touched upon this during a trance talk to two visitors. As usual, his words are applicable to all.

"The world has improved," said Silver Birch, "for one very important reason, and that is the power of the spirit has been at work. Wherever that power finds a lodgment in your world, wherever it is successful in revealing itself through capable instruments, there begins a work of regeneration, and in that work the whole scale of values gradually becomes changed.

"Had it not been for the descent of the power of the spirit in this highly organised form less than a century ago, then indeed the outlook would have been very dire. But the power of the spirit, the great leaven, has been at work throughout the whole of your world. At first there were little drops. Gradually they became streams, then rivers, then seas, and now there is a mighty ocean of the spirit that will never evaporate. That has changed the whole course of history; that has revolutionised the whole outlook of man's life. It has brought the factor of the spirit, the eternal factor, without which all is illogical, unreasonable and without a purpose.

"The whole direction of science, religion, philosophy, art, ethics, morality, music, literature, the whole of life has been changed by the recognition that has gradually been given to the ascendancy of the spirit which rises out of the demonstration that man is a spiritual being who survives the earthly grave. There have been occasional retrogressions, but the march has been onward, and man, slowly, painfully, has evolved towards the light."

"On the other hand," said one of the visitors, "if this planet were very much better than it is, it would cease to have any purpose, because it would not be training us to get to a higher sphere. Therefore, there must be this suffering to cause progress."

"Yes," replied the guide, "but once man is aware of his spiritual nature, once he has caught glimpses of the eternal reality, once he has seen, no matter how faintly, part of the cosmic plan, and realises his place in an infinite scheme of which he is an integral part, then he knows that he, too, is infinite with an infinity of life in which to develop his infinite character. By that I mean that there is an infinite road of progress revealed—the summit cannot be seen for always you are ascending. Do I make myself clear?"

"Perfectly clear. But if this planet was very much better, it would not be a training ground for the spirit. We have to start from the bottom, as I see it, and overcome every experience until we get back to the Great Spirit."

"We are touching vast and profound subjects," said the guide. "We are all part of the Great Spirit, and you in your totality and the totality of all life comprise the Great Spirit. Apart from the totality of life, the Great Spirit has no existence. Now this must be to you purely debatable, because I cannot prove it. Therefore, at the best you can but accept my word for it.

"The road of progress is infinite. Being infinite, there is no finality. Once you have grasped that you will see that there is no merging of ultimates, because if you could reach the stage where the whole of your individuality—not the small fraction that is expressed through the physical body, but the whole of your individuality—could achieve perfection, then the plan of life would cease to be rational.

"Life is infinite, and while you are constantly striving towards perfection, gradually discarding in each phase of your evolution one more fragment of imperfection, the process is an infinite one to which there is no end."

Then one of the visitors asked: "Has the mechanical age helped evolution? It does not look like it."

"In the end it does," answered Silver Birch. "You must see evolution as something which is not a straight line. It is a series of advances and retreats. Man rises and falls, man struggles to rise again and rises higher than he fell, and so gradually, the race evolves. You can point to epochs and say, 'Look! That is a dark stain in evolution.' But that is not the whole story; it is but a part of it.

"The human spirit is gradually evolving, and with that evolution there comes the obvious lesson that is learned as more and more understand the nature of their own beings, as more and more realise their own possibilities, as more and more know the plan of existence and strive to fit themselves into it.

"Centuries ago there were but a handful who dreamed dreams and saw visions. Now the vision splendid has come to hundreds of thousands, and there are countless numbers of reformers, pioneers, teachers, all at work because they know what could be and they desire to help to achieve it. That is where the growth has been made."

"In that I entirely agree with you," said one of the guests. "There is growth, but this planet as a whole, if it were very much better, would not permit of growth."

"But as you grow," explained the guide—"I do not mean you individually, I mean the race—so you will find that the world in which you live can be developed, too, and that you can have a richness of life such as you never before dreamed possible. You speak about the age of the machine, but all the problems arise because man is the slave and not the master. But when he is the master then he can have anything—the age of culture, of leisure, of artistic accomplishment, of the pursuits of the mind and the spirit, and riches of the inner life would be the possession of vast numbers.

"The power lies within each one because each is part of the Great Spirit; the same power that created the whole universe; the same power that fashioned the mountains and stars and planets; the power that gave the sun its light; the power that gave all the perfume to the flowers; the power that made the whole of the universe is within you and you could bring it into activity if you chose to attune yourselves by your life to that great over-ruling force."

"I suppose it is also," said a sitter, "the power that gave perfume to flowers gave poison to the snakes."

"But," countered the guide, "it is all the same thing to me. You know, I never say that the Great Spirit is responsible for all that you call good, and that the devil is responsible for all that you call bad."

"Potentially," added the same questioner, "we have in us all that is good and all that is bad, too."

"Every human being is a microcosm," was the reply. "In miniature, you are the universe. There is potentially the perfection of angelhood and potentially the foulness of the worst brutish beast. That is why you have the free will to develop the path along which you will go.

"I look around your world, torn as it is by war and misery, by chaos and confusion, by distress and sadness, and think there is much to cause the heart to ache. Yet I do not abandon my hope because I know the power of the spirit is at work, that all this is a world in travail, that out of the suffering there will emerge, not at once, but there will emerge a much better world for all who dwell in it."

"You are saying that the whole planet is going to be much better," commented one of the visitors. "How are people going to have the suffering and strife to be able to purify their spirits?"

"Because," said Silver Birch, "man is infinite. There will be no transformation in the twinkling of an eye. It is a long road along which you travel, and there will always be the rise and the fall, the advance and the retreat, but each time more progress will be made."

Answering another question, the guide said: "In our world there is a constant discarding of bodies as the soul is ready for the next sphere of life. But try to visualise that these are not planes in the sense of fixed spheres with boundaries, but rather a series of graded lives which blend and merge into one another. Even in your world, although people occupy the same physical level, spiritually they are at entirely different levels and they are living in different worlds."

Another member of the circle put this view forward, "The amount of progress that society has made is just a speck compared with the progress that has yet to be made."

"No, I would not say that," said Silver Birch. "It is small in comparison, but it is progress. You must remember this: you have evolved laws and codes, systems of ethics; you have enriched literature; you have plumbed the depths of the arts; you have fathomed the treasuries of the mind; you have uncovered some of the riches of the spirit.

"All that is due to the long succession of people who have trod your world, who have suffered and toiled, who have made mistakes and blunders, who were part of the maelstrom of which human existence is composed. But taken altogether there has been an advance and man today is richer, not physically, but spiritually and mentally, than those who trod the earth in the earliest days. It must be so."

Later the guide made this comment: "There is much work to be done in spreading the elementary facts among those who are woefully ignorant, who do not even know that they are spiritual beings, and that they will live beyond what is called death. How tragic it is to contemplate the large numbers going through life deaf, dumb and blind to all spiritual reality! That is a great tragedy. And it is to these that our efforts must be directed, for they are the ones who must be prepared, who must be awakened, so that they can begin to fulfil what their lives are intended to be."

Then Silver Birch addressed the second visitor, a fine medium of many years' standing: "Have confidence in that power which has guided you for many years, and it will not fail you. You are surrounded by much love and it will not fail you. It cannot fail you as long as you are faithful to that trust which is reposed in you.

"I cannot begin to describe what the power of the spirit is, how it works, how it is regulated and the laws to which it is subservient. But I do know that if you provide the right conditions, conditions of earnestness, the desire to serve, confidence that rests on knowledge, that power will maintain, will guide you, will uphold you and will enable you to pass through every experience that your world can offer, and help you to attain the goal which has been set for you."

The mediumistic visitor said she had often seen Silver Birch in her home—he had spoken there for some years—and in parting from her, her husband, and the circle he said: "My task has been made easier by the many friends I have made in your world—people who know me not, except as a voice and a personality.

"The love I receive from them helps me. It is the means by

which I am able to continue, for always we think of those who weep and sorrow, who grieve and mourn, who are bewildered and torn with doubt and fear, and we know that we cannot rest until we have brought some touch of assuagement that will ease life for them.

"That is the great task on which we are all engaged, the task which, if properly performed, enables us to be truly the instruments of that great power which holds us in its embrace of love. Your world is ruled, not from below, but from above. Earthly laws are subject to change and to revision, to repeal and to annulment. New laws are constantly devised for new conditions, but the laws of the spirit are unchangeable: they are immutable, they never fail, they have provided for every circumstance.

"Look up, therefore, and know that the power which created those laws, the power which gave the whole of life its direction and purpose, is the power which is round and about you, the power which can be a cloak to shield you in adversity, the power that holds you always in its embrace of eternal love."

Subsequently Silver Birch gave in these words a superb parable on light and darkness:

"Once upon a time the world was very dark, and along came a man with a little torch and he held it aloft, and it cast gleams of light around him.

"And those who dwelt in the darkness were attracted by the gleams of light, and they drew near until the rays were shed upon them.

"Time went by, and the torch began to flicker. And then one who had lived in the darkness of fear and foreboding, which he now knew was part of the darkness, and was killed by the light, grasped the torch and rekindled it with such vigour that now the illumination was cast even wider.

"And so, throughout all ages, someone has arisen to hold

aloft the torch of life, each adding his own lustre to its luminosity, until gradually the light has been spreading in ever-widening circles. At no stage has the torch been allowed to be extinguished.

"That is all. Hold aloft the torch of the spirit; feed it with the lustre of your own souls so that each one of you helps to dissipate and dispel the gloom in which so many needlessly live.

"That is important. The rest of the things that many people worry about do not matter. When all is said and done, the physical body gets excessive attention; the spiritual body and its requirements are very much neglected."

'There are none forgotten'

"Let us attune ourselves to the highest that we can reach. Oh, Great White Spirit, we strive to present Thee as Thou art, the supreme architect of the vast cosmos of life. Thou art the infinite mind behind the universe. Thy love has conceived it, Thy wisdom directs it and Thy laws sustain it.

"We see that every facet of life comes within the domain of Thy natural law which has provided for every circumstance and left nothing to chance. All comes within the scope of the divine government, all that is both inorganic and organic.

"Thou hast filled the universe with individuals who contain a part of Thy divinity so that for ever there shall be expressed the highest that man possesses. For ever there is the tie of the spirit which unites all people to one another and to Thee, the tie that is above all race, nationality, colour, class and creed; it is the enduring tie, the tie that makes them all one in Thy sight.

"There are none forgotten or overlooked, none neglected or beyond the care of Thy love; all who consider that they are lonely do not realise that the wondrous divine law encompasses them and that they can make themselves more accessible to it.

"Once the eyes and ears of the spirit are opened, there floods in upon human beings the beauty and wisdom and richness of the higher life from whence comes all inspiration, all revelation, all wisdom, all knowledge and all love.

"It is part of our labour to make man aware of his own divinity and his own spiritual nature, that he may realise the earth is but his temporary abode, and his eternal home is in a higher sphere, and that the purpose of his earthly pilgrimage is to direct his feet upon those pathways of understanding which will equip and enrich him and make him worthy of his high origin and his noble destiny.

"This is the prayer of Thy Indian servant who seeks to serve."

Chapter Seven

'JEWELS OF SPIRITUAL TRUTH'

"SERVICE is the coin of the spirit. The only religion which I preach is to give service wherever you can. Never mind theology, or creeds, or rituals, or ceremonies or doctrines. Never mind altars or steeples, the stained glass windows, the vestments: never mind all those things. They are of no account."

So said Silver Birch when a young Eighth Army soldier was invited to the circle. An enthusiastic follower of the guide, he argued with comrades about Spiritualism on troopships, in camps . . . and even on the battlefield.

That night the young visitor asked a series of complicated questions which belied his years. Nonetheless, the guide answered all the varied points put to him with his characteristic simplicity, truly a hallmark of Silver Birch's superb teachings.

"You are a soldier," he told the guest, "but there is a greater war for you to fight, and there are great hosts of mighty battalions who will be behind you if you will take your stand and play your part in fighting this war which has been raging for centuries. The call is to service. There are no medals, no badges, no stripes, no ranks, but we can promise victory will come if there is faithfulness and unremitting devotion. Help us to drive out all these evils that afflict the world of matter. Offer us your own life so that we can use you as one more instrument, and if by virtue of what you do one soul is helped, then your life will not have been in vain. That is how we work."

"One individual seems to do so little," said the soldier. "In the Army we can only talk."

"But one individual with the power of the spirit behind him can do a great deal," was the guide's reply. "I speak in no vainglorious spirit, for I am still filled with humility and with pity. I was given what seemed an insuperable task, to find my way, unknown, with no asset but a voice and some simple teachings, to your world, to seek out an instrument and to win by love and reason.

"Yes, one man; it is one man, but with the self-same power of the spirit that is available to all who desire to serve. And despite hardship and difficulties and obstacles of all kinds, I found an instrument. I trained him to my purpose and gradually, by various means, with patience, I gathered together those who could help me, winning each in turn, not by any offer of a reward, but merely inspiring them with the desire to serve. And see, in a few years, the truths of which we are the instruments, the proud instruments, have encircled the whole world.

"There was one man, and his name was Jesus of Nazareth, and he brought a new standard of religion, based on love, to your world.

"There was one man, and his name was Lincoln, and he freed slaves and united a continent.

"Do you want me to cite more examples of what one man can do? Do not despair. Those who are joined with us in this great battle will not lose. There will be occasional reverses, but we are advancing all the time as knowledge chases away ignorance and light drives out the darkness.

"I am an old soul—so it is said. I know what can be done. Let me then speak words of encouragement to you, to drive away any thoughts of despair. Yes, there is work to be done, great work, the labour for which we require willing hands and hearts and minds. Come and work with us. Be tolerant, help others to see and prize the truth which you have gained, and then let the power of the spirit work its potency on them, and you will see the transformation gradually taking place.

"That is the way it must be done—no mass conversions, no spell-binding evangelism, but truth winning devotees by reason, wisdom, logic, common sense, and, above all, by love. That, in the end, is the only way. Do you not agree?"

"I agree," said the soldier, "but it is going to take a long, long time."

"Somebody has said," remarked Silver Birch, "the world was here before you came and the world will still be here when you have left it. The most that you can do is to make your passage through it worth while. If you help one soul, then you have not failed."

"But, think of all those who go through life and give no service at all," said the visitor.

"All young men are impatient, but the law is evolution, not revolution," replied Silver Birch. "I never curb zeal or enthusiasm, but I do point to the facts as I have found them. Let experience be your guide. That is how and why we can help you. And the truth is that we have made more progress than many realise.

"The power of the spirit is at work all over your world. Lives are being transformed, knowledge is spreading and knowledge is the most potent influence that we can bring to bear. Help to make the children of the Great Spirit free by teaching them to sever the bonds that keep them in prison.

"Do not despair. We will never fail you. That is no boast. With all the knowledge of spiritual law we will bring to bear all the resources of spirit power, which are infinite. And no matter what circumstance may avail you, we will strive to guide and uphold and to sustain you so that you will learn how to overcome them, to tread that path which will lead you to give the greatest service of which you are capable.

"Give service, that is religion. Help the world in which you live, help to enlighten it; be tolerant, kindly, sympathetic; but at the same time fight all evil wherever it rears its head.

"Those are the simple truths which I have returned to enunciate, and as long as you hold on to those simple truths you will not go wrong. Offer knowledge wherever you can. Sometimes it will be rejected and you will be met with scoffing, with ridicule, with mockery. That does not matter. It should not touch you. Those who are unready are perforce unreceptive, but you have done your task.

"But you will meet many to whom this will be precious drops of water when their souls are parched. Those are the ones that matter, and, if you help them, then at least you have justified your existence.

"I want you to take from me the knowledge of what goes on behind physical life, all that vast power of the spirit which is surging around you, of the many influences for good which strive to use you. I want you to try to understand the potentialities of your own self so that you can have access to the vast armouries and riches of your own spiritual nature. I want you to realise that wisdom, divine wisdom, is inexhaustible, that the treasuries of the Great Spirit are infinite.

"We cannot bring you gold, silver or precious stones, but we can bring you the infinitely richer jewels of spiritual truth. They will be untarnished, they will endure for ever. With this to guide you, you have a shining illumination to direct you throughout all life."

Here the Eighth Army soldier said to Silver Birch: "When we were abroad, we were fighting an enemy who, we thought, was wrong. We found that the men who constituted the enemy, the individual soldier, believed in the ideal that he was fighting for. How would he be dealt with as far as laws of retribution are concerned? We believe that he is doing wrong, he believes that he is doing right."

The guide replied: "You must always remember that we do not look on your world through the eyes of your world, that we do not judge according to earthly standards of judgement, that we are not involved in your hatreds and your passions and that we are not subjected to the temporary blindness that so often beclouds your judgement.

"Further, that with some experience of the workings of the law in the world we inhabit, we do not have the same regard for the problems that afflict you, nor do we see them in the same perspective as you do.

"With that very necessary preamble, I must say to you that the overwhelming consideration is the one of motive. He who honestly thinks that he is doing right has committed no offence against his soul. He who knows he is doing wrong and persists, obviously commits that offence because he is cramping his own spirit and affecting its own evolution. We do not see a world of nationalities as you do, we see a race of spiritual beings and we know that each is judged, not by national, but by natural laws."

The soldier's next question was: "How can we decide right from wrong? Is it a matter for the individual or a matter laid down in spiritual laws?"

Silver Birch replied: "It is for the individual, for each one possesses the infallible monitor within his own being. I have had this point presented to me on many occasions and always have I refused to budge one iota from the stand I have adopted.

"I say, with all my knowledge of spiritual law, that every normal individual, that is one who is not deranged or afflicted by mental disease, every normal individual has an infallible index to his own thinking and behaviour; that is his conscience —his inexorable guide to all that he thinks, says and does, and automatically, instinctively, on every occasion, whatever your problem or perplexity, your own conscience unhesitatingly tells you whether you are right or wrong.

"Sometimes you strive to stifle it, sometimes you seek to argue it away by temporising and by discussion, but always, within yourself, you know."

Silver Birch commented, after a discussion of a complex problem:

"I am a very practical being. I always refuse to be led on to intricate paths which I think will not help your world in its present plight. I see that it requires fundamental knowledge, the knowledge that will enable it to reshape the whole of its systems so that it can get rid of all the present squalor and dirt and slums and inequality and injustice, all of which are preventing the spirit of man from finding expression.

"When I look around your world and see what could be a wondrous garden choked with all the dirty, dank weeds that prevent any flower from finding its expression of beauty, then I say to you, attack these fundamental problems, wage your war on the enemy which is much stronger than any foe you have at present met on fields of warfare.

"Fight the enemy who keeps the human spirit in subjection; fight the enemy who oppresses the human spirit and keeps the soul in bondage. Fight all those who deny man his elementary rights to have the sunshine, to have the freedom which is part of his divine heritage.

"These are the first problems that await your attention. And if you can inspire that zeal and enthusiasm in all those whom you know and who think that this knowledge can help them, then tell them that its primary purpose is not to satisfy philosophical speculation, but to make your world a kingdom of heaven on earth, so that man learns his lessons there and does not come to us in that dreadful condition in which many are arriving today."

The soldier commented: "I agree, but when you look at places like India and see people there with not enough food or clothing, it is rather bewildering . . ."

Silver Birch answered: "No, it is not so terrific, if you will allow the voice and the power of the spirit to guide and uphold you, if you will rid your world of the curse of creedalism which holds so many in chains, which encourages rancour and bitterness and hatred, which defeats the children of the Great Spirit, which makes them live in the foul, inky blackness of superstition and prejudice and ignorance.

"If you will teach them how to be free and banish all those ancient myths and fables which have been called religion for too long and tell them how they can have the sunlight of spiritual truth; if you will drive away all that falsity and error that has come in the name of religion, you will begin to solve many of the problems of your world. I tell you with all the solemnity of which I am capable that your world has been cursed by creedalism."

Here the soldier asked, "How about the economic side?"

And the guide replied: "It is all part of the same problem. I am a disturber. I am told that I preach doctrines which are not in accordance with the tenets of Christianity, and yet I think I know more about Christianity than those who criticise me. All your problems resolve themselves into the one simple fact—man is a spiritual being and by virtue of his heritage possesses certain fundamental rights.

"Those rights are that the spirit shall find the richness of expression in an earthly world to qualify it for its next stage of life. Anything which stands in the way must be overthrown; that is all. You may call it whatever name you choose. I am not concerned with labels or with parties. I am concerned with truth.

"If you were to see, as I do, day after day, souls arriving in our world stunted, thwarted, misshapen, unevolved, unready, then you would be filled, as I am, with the desire to so transform the whole of your world so that it should not happen again.

"Rejoice that, at so young an age, you have found knowledge to guide you. Many others regret that this knowledge came to them in the winter of their earthly lives and you are but at the spring. You have yet to attain the summer of your fulfilment."

And with these words the guide ended the interview:

"Let us pause to remember the power which is round and about each one of us, a power guided by love and wisdom that sustains us and wraps us in its garment.

"Let us strive by our actions to be worthy of the trust reposed in each one of us and do nothing to dishonour the mission on which we are engaged.

"Let us always determine to be valiant soldiers for truth, determined to fight wherever we can give service.

"Let us never be weary in well-doing and strive to offer ourselves as instruments for that power which is always at work, striving to spread truth wherever it can."

Another time Silver Birch answered questions put to him by a young American soldier, whose brother had recently passed on. His first point, said the guest, was very simple. Hannen Swaffer had told him that when he first manifested Silver Birch had difficulty speaking English. So what language did the guide originally speak? The guide replied:

"You see here a physical body—this that you call a medium, for the word means an intermediary, someone who is the instrument through whom something is sent. Now, there are various strata of life in our world. It is a world which is regulated by the spiritual growth of those who dwell in it. It is a graded life and in each grade—they all merge into one another—there are those who have attained that spiritual growth which enables them to dwell in that sphere or state or being.

"The longer you have lived in our world the further you are divorced from your world and the ties have become more or less sundered.

"I had attained some degree of spiritual growth in that time, and a call was made for many of us to return to help your world to teach some of the eternal verities, simple truths, principles, which had been forgotten, overlaid, which lay buried beneath a debris of falsity, superstition, ignorance, misconception and prejudice.

"In order to teach your world, I had to reduce my normal rate of vibration—that is the easiest way of explaining it to you—and in doing so sacrificed some of my individuality, for the nearer you come to earth, the less of the real you, the spiritual you, can be made manifest, and in order to achieve communication with your world I had to use a medium between my state of existence and yours.

"Now the language I speak in my own state, to which I occasionally return, is not the language of earth at all. We do not require your symbols in the world where I belong, but, to make myself understood in your world, I had to master your language.

"I was helped by those whom I regard as specialists and expert in it."

"Where did you come from originally when you were on earth?" asked the American, who was told:

"That does not matter. You will have to accept what I say if it appeals to your reason. If anything I say to you seems to outrage your common sense, reject it. If anything which comes to you through the lips of any instrument sounds to you as being unworthy of the source of its origin, do not accept it.

"I have been at work for many years in your world and I

had to start with the handicap that I could only make my way by the reasonableness of the principles which I taught. These I am prepared to enunciate and to reason with anybody.

"I cannot claim to have any authority other than that which is contained in the truth of that which I teach. I claim that all these teachings bear the hall-mark of their own spiritual authenticity, that if they are subject to the analysis of reason, wisdom, common sense, they will pass all those tests and what is there is a philosophy, a truth, which will enable your world to find abiding peace, to banish the hatred, chaos, misery, iniquity, selfishness and all the evils which, alas, are far too prevalent.

"If I say to you I am Julius Caesar, that would not make what I say any more or less acceptable. The truth must be tested and established by the fact that it is true, not because it was uttered by one who has been invested with an aura of glory."—"You say that you speak a different language from where you come . . ."

"You are putting questions to me, and what you are doing is first of all to have a thought in your mind. That thought is quite clear to your consciousness. You know what you are thinking, but to convey that thought to me you have to use a symbol, a symbol which has a meaning to others who understand that symbol. That symbol you call language, and the words you use consist of attempts to clothe your thought in a manner that will make the thought understandable.

"Your mastery over the language will determine whether you have suitably or unsuitably expressed the thought which is in your mind. But even if you had the mastery of a Shakespeare it would still be insufficient to express the totality of your thought, for your thought is immaterial and your language is material. The one who hears these symbols, has, in turn, to translate them back into their original thought-form before he appreciates them, so that there is a long and cumbersome process at work.

"And often, because you have to materialise your thoughts, there is much friction, misunderstanding, simply because the words do not always convey what you have thought."

"That is very true," commented the soldier. Silver Birch continued: "Now if it were possible for you, without an intermediary of language, to convey the totality of your thought to another person, most of the problems, or rather many of the problems, which worry your world would disappear, for there would be no misunderstanding, no misconception, you would all know what you meant, there would be an end to all the vast diplomacy, all the needless equivocation.

"In my world our language is the language of thought; that is, we communicate with one another, once we have outgrown earthly habits, by mental communication, so that the language bar is no complication. A Frenchman can communicate with a Swede and an Eskimo with an Italian. It is the thoughts they are sending to one another, not the words, which are the symbol of the thought. That is quite clear, I hope."

"Yes, I understand," said the visitor. "Now there are people who have passed away from this earth. Suppose we take musicians; could a person who passed away recently communicate with someone who passed away years and years ago?"

"Not necessarily," answered the guide. "It depends on several factors. You must not think of yourself as a body with a spirit, but as a spirit with a body. You are living in a material world and are apt to think of the whole of life in material terms, but life is not material in essence, for the foundation and basis of life is immaterial. Its origin is not to be found in any of the properties of matter. You yourself are not material; your body is, but the real you is at present impalpable, unseen, intangible, unheard; the real you is a spirit.

"The quality of your spirit at any moment is determined by the way that you have lived your life. Thus the law applies to all and none has the power to thwart it. When I say the law, I mean the natural law, for the law is simply one of cause and effect.

"If you live a life of complete selfishness, you yourself are the one who bears the result of it, for a selfish life means a stunted spirit. If you have lived a kindly, tolerant, altruistic life, you yourself are the better for it, for your spirit has grown in stature. This law applies to all.

"You are what you make yourself to be by your own conduct, by your own actions, by your own thought, by the whole of your life. And although that reality may not be visible in your world, the moment you pass the threshold of death, severing yourself from your physical body, you manifest as you spiritually are—no higher, no lower.

"You take with you just that character which you have moulded by your life. Your eternal possessions are the spiritual qualities that you have evolved by your daily life. That is why the law is so fair and so just, for it provides a standard of judgement about which no reasonable man could quarrel . . . Your associates are those of like spiritual growth and like spiritual mentality."

"In other words," said the American, "someone of another age but of the same spiritual mentality would be in the same spirit sphere."

"Yes, that is so. It is not governed by years, it is not governed by physical age: it is governed wholly and solely by spiritual growth. And that is the tremendous difference between your world and our world.

"Here you are apparently on the same physical plane, meeting and mingling with people who are on different mental planes to yourself. In our world you are with those who are on the same spiritual altitude as yourself. That does not mean to say that you cannot hear famous musicians, but your life is lived amongst your spiritual equals, and that is determined by the law of spiritual gravitation which is infallible . . .

"Try to realise this. Your world for centuries has become coarsened through its materialism. Originally mankind was able to function on many planes of activity.

"Man was aware of the gifts of the spirit which are merely the expressions of the faculties that belong to his inner eternal reality. If you examine the records of the past, if you turn to your Bible, for example—although I do not confine myself to that book—you will find that the more you go back to primitive times, the more natural was the exercise of these psychic faculties. But, like all other faculties, they have atrophied through long disuse and the number of those today who can register the vibrations of the spirit is very, very small.

"You, all of you, are living in prisons. You have five tiny windows to your prison, and these five apertures are your physical senses. You are unaware of the millions of happenings around you unless they can be seen, smelt, touched, tasted or felt. But because you do not see the busy, teeming, active world around you, that does not mean to say it has no existence. It means only one thing, that you are unable to register its vibration.

"What you call death is the stilling of the physical body; it drops away unfortunately too often before the spirit is prepared, but once death takes place you are liberated, for your spirit leaves the prison of the physical body and expresses itself through that finer body, the body of the spirit, your etheric body, as it is sometimes called, which has been preparing itself for this dissolution. Once you are dead—as your world calls it—you have access to a far greater range, a range of life's activity, than you had before because the whole realm of psychic faculty begins to work."

"Another point," said the visitor. "You speak of 'your world' and the Church says there is another world; do spirit beings stay in the same place as when they lived here, or have they an entirely new existence?"

"It is all one universe with many worlds in it," said the guide. "All life is one life, but it has many gradations. I am confronted with the difficulty of language to explain spiritual realities and so when I have recourse to these crude, clumsy and inadequate symbols, I am unable to convey all that I intend.

"Life is one, the universe is one, there is no boundary, there is no frontier. Those who have passed from your ken are in the same universe as you are, but they are registering different vibrations, they are functioning on a different plane or aspect of consciousness. But they are here, even though you cannot see them, just as much as you are in our world even though you cannot know it.

"All aspects of life blend into one another. There is no boundary—on one side there is the material and on the other side the spiritual world. It is an intermingling. It is like the vibrations of the wireless which fill all space: there are different wave-lengths, different vibrations, but they are all occupying the same space at the same time.

"And the ability to tune in to different vibrations depends upon the sensitiveness of the instrument. You are restricted to the vibrations of matter, that is all you can register. The medium who is clairvoyant is able to register finer vibrations of light, the medium who hears registers finer and more subtle vibrations of sound. It depends upon the range of the instrument.

"At first you must remember those who come to our world,

to our state of life, to the realm of spirit, are bewildered. They are unprepared, and naturally the gravitational pull of earth attracts them because all their love, all their life, all their consciousness, all their memories, all their associations are on earth.

"For a long time they hover around those scenes where they have spent many years, bewildered because they have not realised that they are what you call dead, confused because they can make no impression on material objects or attract the attention of people in their old home or business or factory.

"But gradually awareness comes and they realise that they are manifesting but another aspect of consciousness."

"Lots of times I wish that my brother were here; that he could see the things that I see," commented the visitor.

"Yes, he can," said the guide.

"I have no way of knowing that he is there?"

"No, unfortunately," said Silver Birch, "unless you develop your psychic power so that you can see him and receive communication from him yourself. He is aware of you all the time because he has added faculties which you do not possess. But you are not aware of him because you have not developed the faculties that would give you this awareness."

"You say develop my psychic gifts as if I had psychic gifts," said the soldier.

"Yes, you have," said Silver Birch. "Everyone has psychic faculties. I realise that this is very revolutionary. I know that when you allow your mind to dwell on it you will see that this is the fundamental truth which was taught by all those whose names are identified with religion in your world.

"This is the fundamental truth enshrined in the teachings of all the great religious teachers, for each of them was subject to this same common inspiration. It all comes from the same divine reservoir, and all of them taught these selfsame spiritual truths—that man is a spiritual being with a spiritual destiny to achieve and that he is placed on earth to equip himself for the greater life that awaits him and that he takes with him the love that he has earned, the character that he has built, the spiritual gifts he has cultivated.

"Is that not the central teaching of all religions, and is it not true that this central teaching has been forgotten in all religions, without exception? It has been replaced by a mass of doctrine, of theology, of creedalism, of man-made ideas which have no connection with religion and which have no value as a religion at all."

Answering another question the guide said: "I say to you as I say to all those who know me, and you, of course, do not know me very well: do that which you think is right always. Never mind what the world says, never mind what those around you say; do that which you think is right, not that which is convenient or expedient, but that which you think within yourself when you know, when the inner conviction forces it on you that it is right to adopt a certain course.

"It is very simple, but unfortunately your world will not listen to simplicity; it prefers complexity and intricacy. It is suspicious of the simple which has become almost platitudinous.

"I urge upon all to follow their conscience, for I know that the conscience is the divine monitor within man—the means of assessing right from wrong, the means of establishing the paths which should be followed. Once the voice of conscience dictates its action you should follow it unerringly, without question, no matter what difficulties may loom up, for in the end it will lead you right.

"That is very simple. I cannot put it simpler than that.

"You are not very old as your world considers age. You have certain advantages and certain handicaps, but, like everybody else, you have certain talents. I can only say to you, use those talents to help others. You are living in a world which is full of tears and misery and sorrow and sadness. Try to help those less fortunate than yourself.

"Look around and see the millions who yearn for some comfort, some guidance, some light in their weary perplexity. You may be able to help some of them.

"There are too many who are victims of circumstances over which they have no control; too many who are underfed, who live in squalor, who are subject to dirt, disease, who have not had a fair chance, whose spirits are compelled to try to express themselves through cramped, restricted, thwarted bodies.

"You may be able to help some of them, who knows? For those are the things which are important. It is what you do that matters and believe me—believe this if you believe nothing else—if you have helped one soul to find the light, if you have given food to one who was hungry or drink to one who was thirsty, if you have helped to ease the burden on someone's shoulders and to smooth the stones in front of their path, that is more important than all the wealth in your world.

"Try to acquire knowledge of spiritual realities. Too many, alas, go through your life living in the shadows of darkness, a darkness which some of us are trying to pierce with a little illumination of spiritual truth.

"The darkness need not be, for your world could be a veritable Kingdom of Heaven on earth. It only needs the service of those who understand to minister to the ones who have fallen or who are too weak.

"I try to encourage all to serve, for to me service is the only religion in the world. I care not for hymns, for bibles, for churches, for chapels; these are unimportant unless they encourage people to make your world better than it is. True religion is to serve your fellow-men wherever you can.

"Never mind who I am; that does not matter. I may be someone who was important. I may be someone who was insignificant in your world. Titles and names do not count. If

I can express any truth which helps you, then I rejoice, for I am fulfilling the purpose of my being, which is to try to serve your world.

"But whether I have succeeded or not," said the guide, as the seance came to an end, "may I try to leave one thought with you and it is just this: remember there are around and about you many unseen presences whose one desire is to guide you, to guard you and to influence you along the lines of the greatest good.

"You are never lonely, you are never neglected. Always there are those whose mantle of love is wrapped around you, and the power which they wield is the power of the spirit, that power which is the genesis of all life, the power that fashioned the sun, the moon, the stars, the mountains, the oceans, the whole of life, the whole universe and all that it contains."

'The fountain of divine wisdom'

"Oh Great White Spirit, we strive to reveal glimpses of Thy infinite wisdom, Thy infinite knowledge and Thy infinite love.

"Throughout all the centuries, those who have been possessed with the open vision have caught glimpses of the larger, fuller, deeper life, and have interpreted it in the language, customs and characteristics of their day.

"Always there have been witnesses of Thy eternal truths, men and women who have known of the existence of the power of the spirit, for it had moved them and made them aware of its fine, delicate and subtle vibrations. But, inevitably, all this inspiration has become tainted and overgrown.

"So, once again, we who are Thy servants, Thy messengers, seek to reveal that eternal truth, this time in all its pristine beauty and simplicity, not as part of any special dispensation, not as an event unique in history, not as a miraculous occurrence, but as part of Thy natural law.

"We desire to reveal that, beyond the world of matter and all its confines, there is a vast, active realm of spirit, where people, still Thy children, who, having evolved and drawn nearer to the fountain of divine wisdom, wish to impart all that they have learned to minds and hearts and souls which are receptive.

"Thus, there will be an ever-growing number of Thy children conscious of this impact from the higher world, ready to act as its instruments, to spread its light, its knowledge, its comfort, its power and its guidance. We desire to extend this ministry far and wide, so that constantly there is drawn within the radius of spirit power an ever-increasing number of channels which can be used to give service to the ones who need it most.

"We see a growing suffering, large numbers of those filled with pain and anxiety, whose eyes are beclouded with tears of sorrow, whose hearts are heavy with anguish and suffering, who feel that they are lonely, and that there is no hope, no comfort in a drear and darkened world.

"It is to these that we direct our message. It is these we seek to touch, so that they may become assured of Thy infinite laws, Thy infinite love and Thy infinite power, that they may know Thou hast not forgotten them and that within Thy kingdom there is ample provision for all Thy children.

"That is the task to which we have dedicated ourselves, which we share with many who desire to relieve suffering, to allay anxiety, to help those who mourn and who are distressed from any cause, so that they may be brought out of the darkness towards the light.

"That is the prayer of Thy Indian servant who seeks to serve."

Chapter Eight

'THE TRUTH SHALL SPREAD'

THROUGHOUT the many long years of his earthly mission, Silver Birch never once displayed annoyance, impatience or irritation. Neither did he judge those who came to hear him speak. Truly was he a wise, old, benevolent soul.

There came an evening when a visitor told the guide: "I want to believe. In a way I have always believed . . ." What followed from a so-called dead Red Indian was an answer which is in essence a perfect summary of the case of Spiritualism.

"It is part of our task to bring knowledge to your world," Silver Birch began. "We are entrusted with a great mission. Many people on my side of life have seen that there is too much ignorance on earth. The results of that ignorance are, alas, all too apparent. It is reflected in the misery of your world, and it is also reflected in the misery of ours. The churches have painted a picture of people passing through the gates of death and immediately being transformed into radiant beings filled with indescribable happiness, having left behind them all the worries and cares and anxieties. But that is not so. It is far from being a true picture.

"People who die are—in the early stages—just the same as those who live. They have shed a physical body, that is all. They have not changed their individuality; their character is not altered. Their habits and traits and idiosyncrasies and characteristics remain just as they were; the selfish still selfish, the greedy still greedy, the ignorant still ignorant, the deluded still deluded, until the process of spiritual awakening takes place.

"This happened so many times that in our world there came the determination to fill the earth with some knowledge of reality. And so, for many years, people like myself have been entrusted with the task of trying to tell the truth about the spiritual life, not in any mystical sense as the phrase so often conveys, but what it is in reality. We have had to undo generations and generations of misrepresentation, ignorance, prejudice, lies, deception, superstition, all the forces which have held millions of people in the darkness of subjection.

"We have allied ourselves into one vast army with the object of bringing spiritual liberation to those who have been held in captivity for too long. What we have to say is very simple. It begins first with a demonstration. It is that we declare that all can be proven by every individual who sets out with an honest purpose, freed from bias, with a desire to know the truth. Those who love you will prove their presence, despite the incident of death, if you give them the opportunity and provide them with the right channels.

"That is not a fantastic speculation, it is a cold, calm statement of something which has been proved many, many hundreds of thousands of times. It is beyond the realm of disputation or controversy, except for those who are blind because they do not wish to see, or for those whose minds are so distorted that they can no longer recognise the truth when it stands in front of them.

"That is the first purpose, to provide a demonstration of spiritual truth, to meet the challenge of a materialistic world which says: 'Prove it. We cannot believe any more; for too long we have been asked to believe in fantasy, in irrational doctrine, that we have turned our backs and we ask for that which we can assess, judge, measure, weigh, analyse, dissect.'

"The answer has been fully given. It is there; each individual can have it for himself. That is the foundation on which we build the rock of certainty which has stood and will stand all the assaults that have been made upon it. No longer is it a question of saying, 'I believe, I have faith, I have hope.' There are millions who can say: '*I know*. This fact has been established.'

"For the first time in the history of your world religion has been built on a bedrock of certainty. Men may argue about theological dogmas which none can prove, but of human survival there is proof sufficient to satisfy all reasonable men. But that is only the beginning; it is not the end. It is necessary for those who do not know to have this demonstration; it is necessary for them to be satisfied that the main basis is true.

"There is a life beyond the grave. The dead, as you call them, survive. They can and they do return, but it is not the end. Why have they survived, what is the manner of their survival, what is the effect of their earthly lives upon the new life which they began after death? What is the relationship between these two states of being? What experiences have they had since they passed through the gates of death? Have they been helped or hindered by what they did or said or thought?

"What lessons have they learned that they can pass on? What are the things that endure when all material possessions have been left behind? What is the effect of this demonstration on religion, on science, on politics, on economics, on art, on international relationships, on the colour question? Yes, they are all affected, for the new knowledge brings a new illumination to old problems that have vexed a tortured humanity for many ages."

Asked whether that outline had helped her, the guest replied, "It has simplified things a great deal for me."

The guide continued: "I tell you one other thing. In addition to this constant war we wage on all the forces of darkness and reaction and on all those who have a vested interest in darkness and reaction, we also wage war on fear.

"There are certain conditions which make the association

between you and us, in the broad sense, that is, between you and those you love in my world, easier or harder. There is a barrier which can be broken down, a barrier of misunderstanding and hostility and ignorance, and it is easiest for us to manifest our presence when you are in a certain frame of mind and spirit. You are spirits in a physical body. We are spirits without physical bodies. There is a nexus, something which is common to us both—the tie of the spirit.

"You are spiritual beings here and now in your world. You do not become spiritual beings because you die. It is not death which confers upon you a spiritual body. Death merely releases you from the prison of the flesh and you are liberated just as much as a bird when you open the cage and set it free.

"You have, in essence, all the gifts, attributes and qualities of the spirit that you will ever have. They are now within you, latent, unexpressed, except perhaps in matters of small degree. You can learn how to give them a richer expression, how to allow the real you to manifest itself, how to allow the larger self to come into its own and to begin to claim part of its wondrous heritage. In all forms of communication with your world, those who come back to you must, of necessity, make some little sacrifice, for they have to come down to lower vibrations, they have to transmute the spiritual into the material to reach you.

"Most of you, the majority of mankind, are incapable of aspiring to the heights of the spirit. They cannot register the vibrations of the spirit; these vibrations are too delicate, too sensitive, too rarefied to be caught except by a comparative few. So, those who wish to manifest to you have to come down in the scale, as it were, and, in doing so, naturally, much of the beauty has to be lost. It would be better if you could meet them halfway, if you could rise in the scale; then you would enjoy something far richer than is yet known. But you are still spiritual beings. If you allow the spirit to express itself, to radiate, it loses all things like fear and doubt. The spirit lives in an atmosphere of confidence.

"The enemy on which we wage war is needless fear that is harboured in so many minds. We see millions afflicted with worries that do not always exist except in their imagination, and so I stress again and again, get rid of fear. There is no problem with which you are confronted that is beyond you. There is no difficulty that cannot be mastered. There is no load so heavy that it cannot be borne, and if you live and breathe an atmosphere of radiant confidence, you will attract all the forces that can help you and guide you and sustain you.

"You must try to realise that this is a very, very large and comprehensive subject, for we touch every facet of life and that therefore, to you who are in the initial stages, there is the joy to be experienced of exploration, of finding new spiritual adventures, and I urge you to go ahead."

The visitor asked, "How long does it take before a spirit being comes back to this world after death takes place?"

"It depends on the conditions," said Silver Birch. "There are some who come into our world, who, although they have been here for centuries, have not yet awakened to the realisation of what has taken place."

"They don't know they are dead," commented a member of the circle.

"And there are some," added the guide, "who come here with knowledge, who know the ropes, and to them, if they can find the right medium, they can manifest within a few moments of their passing. There is no simple answer. It is dependent upon the condition of the person himself, whether he has knowledge or ignorance. One of our great difficulties is that many people come here with very strong preconceived ideas of what this world is like. They refuse to believe that it can be anything else than the world that exists in the pictures of their imagination. Because they believe that intently, that is the world in which they live, for you must remember ours is a world of the mind and the spirit, and what you think is your reality."

After Silver Birch had advised a healer in the circle about his work, he said to the visitor: "That is another part of the work, too. Healing forces can be transmitted through earthly channels to bring health to those who are sick. It is a very large subject with many facets and aspects, and I expect some of it is a little bewildering at first, but it is a great truth and once you know it is true your life is transformed.

"In some churches they talk about conversion. They mean by that that you accept some formal declaration, that you say you believe in a certain doctrine—and now you are converted.

"But once the knowledge of spiritual truth has succeeded in finding a lodgment within your being you become transformed. You look at life through new eyes, with a new confidence, a new understanding, for its purpose begins to take shape and you realise something of the plan which the Great Spirit has for all His children.

"Some are inspired to work in the fields of political activity, to transform this knowledge so as to raise the standard of the suffering and the victimised, the helpless and the betrayed. Others go into the field of religion to attempt to resuscitate the old bones of theology. Others go into the laboratories of science to bring these new ideas of life to those who have been led into channels which, alas, become blind alleys. Others go into the fields of art.

"The truth is that it touches every phase of life, for life is spirit and spirit is life. Once the spirit is awake and has become aware of itself, once the consciousness has dawned, then you know who you are, what you are, why you are and you should spend the rest of your life in helping to equip yourself by service for the richer and the greater life that is your inevitable destiny.

"Go on questing. Always ask, for you do receive. Never is a response refused from our world, although sometimes it is not the answer which you want but the answer that is best suited to your development."

At a further sitting, Silver Birch touched upon the task confronting all Spiritualists. He said:

"Let us remember the vast field of labour in which we work. You are living in times of sore distress when many souls are grievously troubled, when many hearts are filled with despair, when many backs groan under the burden which they have to carry. There are millions who know not where to turn, who think that life is bereft of all hope, who cry out for some gleam to come to them. There is much that we have to offer—the riches of the spirit. With loyalty, with trust, with confidence, with steadfastness, with determination, with resolve, we can help some, and more than that no one can do.

"Let us always remember that we are the instruments of a greater and higher purpose that seeks to use us, each one of us. Let us realise that we are the vessels and that there can be poured through us the balm that will satisfy and assuage grief. Let us remember that there is a power, infinite in its purpose, that is at our disposal, and that this power, the power of the spirit, is capable of solving every problem with which mankind is confronted."

Silver Birch referred to his activities in the higher spheres since he had last spoken at this circle. "As always," he said, "the prospect of returning to the world of matter is not altogether one that is joyful, but conscious of the tasks imposed on us and the help given by your love, I come back to do what little I can to help those who need it and who will accept it.

"I have spent quite a long time with those who were my associates in the sphere of life that is my natural habitat and it seems that, so far as I can ascertain, there is no dissatisfaction at what we have managed to achieve by our efforts. There is no reason to assume that, with continued loyalty, fidelity and co-operation, we shall fail, as the plan begins further to reveal itself.

"We cannot measure the extent to which the power of the spirit is penetrating everywhere. We who are engaged in this task, and hear only of the immediate happenings and circumstances in our own field, do not know, neither can we be expected to know, whether the efforts that are made are as far-reaching as it was supposed they would be. We just go on with our task, helping wherever we can, wondering sometimes whether many or few are reached thereby. But those who gather up all the threads, those who meet in concert from time to time, and know by various means of the reactions in all parts of the world, they are the ones who can assess and gauge the effect of what is being done.

"Beyond the confines of our knowledge there is a transformation slowly taking place. There is an ever-growing lightening of the gloom; the fog continues to be dissipated; slowly the mists begin to roll away. More and more find that they are no longer bound and shackled and fettered. They taste the air of freedom. They begin to realise what it is to live, mentally and spiritually, in an atmosphere where there is no fear, no terror. They begin to know and to understand that they are not alone, neglected, forgotten, that the hand of infinite love is stretched out and that it has touched them. They are reassured, they feel that life is worth-while once again. In many places of your world there are such individuals who can say that today, but they could not have said it yesterday.

"That is the measure of our progress, the souls who are released from thraldom, the ones who do not weep any more, unless it be that they weep tears of gratitude; the ones who have been made whole in body and mind; the ones who are no longer racked in agony; the ones who have escaped from all the servitude created by false creed and doctrine; the ones who live in liberty, conscious of the majesty of the power of the spirit. This is the result of our labour, and the labour of all like us, whose lives are dedicated to the ennobling task of enfranchisement. There are still millions to be reached.

"Let us hope and pray and determine that, if it be in our power, we shall succeed in reaching and touching some of them, so that they, too, may find that assurance which they lack and be brought to a realisation of those eternal truths which provide a refuge for all mankind; that they may be able to be aware of that power of the spirit, regenerating in its influence, revitalising in its force, comforting in its presence, ennobling in its purpose; so that they, too, in time, may become its instruments and help to spread its light wider and wider throughout the world."

Then the guide made this statement on the future of Spiritualism and other truths through which mankind learns its spiritual nature:

"It is planned that truth shall spread not through one instrument, but permeate through tens of thousands of instruments all over the world of matter. You must remember that so long as the power of the spirit has been at work man has been on the march. He now begins to claim his heritage, his spiritual freedom. These ideas, these urges, these impulses are so potent that they cannot and will not be denied, and all over your world of matter new ideas are bestirring millions who yearn and claim and demand the liberty of the spirit, of the mind, and of the body.

"That is how your New World will come into fulfilment. Thrones will topple, rulers will fade away, tyrants and dictators will disappear. Man will gradually come into his own, and his spirit will shine triumphant in his life everywhere.

"That is what will be achieved by the surging, rising

impulses of the spirit that are now at work in their great process of regeneration. That is why I never despair, for I see the onward march of the human spirit towards the goal of its liberation."

"We have had enough examples shown to us to work on," remarked a member of the circle.

"Yes, you have the precepts," said the guide, "now you want the performers."

Another time the spirit sage was asked, "Is the development of psychic faculties the next step in man's evolutionary progress?" The guide replied:

"Without question, those who are termed psychic, or mediumistic, are the precursors of evolution. They are the advance guard of the next rung in the ladder of evolution. In time to come, psychic faculties will be part of the normal equipment of human beings. Your world is going through a stage of mental unfoldment, and that is why the unfolding psychic faculty will follow in its trail."

An American visitor asked the guide what he meant by the words "psychic faculties." He answered:

"The ability to receive impressions, vibrations, which are beyond those normally received through the channels of your five perceptions of sense. You must appreciate that man is not an animal confined to five avenues for his sole contacts with the universe. These five windows allow him to know only a small part of universal activity. They limit him to that which can be registered in terms of matter.

"Man is more than matter, man is mind and spirit, and there are vibrations that belong to the mental and spiritual life. In addition, there are vibrations which belong to the superphysical life, the life that is beyond the earthly world. Man can register the vibrations of this life in which he lives, and the vibrations of that larger life which one day will be his eternal habitat."

"Is it possible for you to locate any particular individual in your world?" was the next question.

"It can be done by those who are skilled in the performance of these tasks," was the spirit reply. "You must appreciate that the individuals in our world fall into two categories, those who desire to return and those who do not desire to return. Amongst those who desire to return, it is quite easy to establish contact with your world, provided there is a suitable instrument. Those who do not desire to return can be easily located, but there is nothing that we can do to compel them to return."

Replying to another question, Silver Birch said: "What you must realise is this. There are many intelligences in our world who feel very naturally the attraction of love, affection, friendship and sympathy.

"Wherever there is this bond of the mind or spirit, it is based upon reality, because mental and spiritual forces are stronger than earthly ones. An artist in your world whose whole heart goes out to another artist, perhaps a greater one, who has already passed through the door of death, attracts him, and the artist in my world returns to become an influence because of this bond of attraction.

"What you must appreciate, also, is that whatever qualities of the mind or spirit you possess whilst you are on earth, when you die, as the world calls it, and slough off the physical body, you begin to develop those qualities and become far greater than ever you were on earth. The clamping, restrictive influence of the body has been removed. Where you can find an instrument, a medium, a channel, you do so so that you can share your extended gifts.

"Sometimes this is an unconscious influence. Artists in your world realise that they are the subject of inspiration which is non-physical, but they do not realise that it comes from the world of spirit. In other cases, there is awareness that it is direct inspiration from someone who is regarded as dead.

"In the same way as I, who have learnt just a little more about the laws of life, about spiritual realities, return to share this knowledge with those who are receptive, so greater souls than I desire to do so, because greatness consists in the desire to be of service. You are great, not for what you receive, but for what you give.

"Try to understand that you are all instruments, or could be, of higher beings who strive to use you for the greatest possible good. If you will but say to yourself, 'Whatever gift or talent I have, I place it at the disposal of mankind, to be used to help to alleviate distress, to uplift, to redress wrong, in short, to give service'—if that is your paramount outlook, then you have nothing to fear.

"There is no circumstance that can cross your path and bring any harm to you. With a high purpose to guide you, with an inflexible determination not to turn aside, following, all the time, every precept that urges the greatest good to the greatest number, you cannot go wrong."

The visitor, who was anxious to receive a spirit communication from one individual, was given this advice by Silver Birch on how to sit with a trance medium:

"Whenever you go with a dominant idea, that is an obstacle to communication. Your task at the earthly end of the line is to be receptive, not to bombard the atmosphere with dominant thoughts. The more you throw out the one idea that you want only this and nothing else, the more you have blocked the channel. It is a channel through which many can come, but they can only do so when it is open, and not when it is closed.

"We can reach you when you are in a sympathetic and receptive frame of mind, when you open the door of your mind and soul and say, 'Now I am ready to receive.' If you say, 'I am not ready to receive, I want only this one,' that is restricting the channel and making it difficult even for the one you want."

"Why is it that mediums do not always receive surnames in giving clairvoyance?" was another point addressed to the guide.

"Because, usually, they are more difficult to receive than the other kind," he answered. "It is all a question of the registration of vibration of sounds. Sounds with which they are already acquainted are easier to be transmitted and received. The more unusual and uncommon the name, the harder it is for it to be transmitted and to be received.

"Then again, so much of that which comes from our world is received by mediums in pictorial or symbolic form, and often surnames are almost impossible to transmit in terms of pictures or symbols. But where you have instruments who can see very clearly or hear very clearly, they can succeed in registering surnames. It must be remembered that the acid test of mediumship is not the ability to receive surnames, but the ability to give evidence of discarnate presences."

'We seek to inspire'

"I pray to the Great White Spirit, Whom we seek to reveal as the perfect Law in operation, that we may call down that power that inspired the prophets of old and enabled the sages and seers to present the vision of a world filled with the splendour of Thy wisdom and give them that truth which brought light and understanding and cleared away the shadows that had filled men's minds.

"Once again we seek to resurrect that power which can change the whole course and destiny of human life, which can transform all humankind, give them strength and courage and purpose so that they can understand their place in Thy eternal scheme and work for betterment, for amelioration, for service, to rescue all those who have fallen by the wayside, to give help to the helpless, to succour the hungry, give strength to the weak and to drive out the inequalities that are a curse and a blot on the civilisation of today.

"We seek to bring man to those paths which lead to a fuller understanding of Thee and of themselves, so that they may turn their backs on false gods, false creeds, false theologies and, following the light of Thy truth, may establish that religion which is worldwide and universal in its application, so that all Thy children may worship together in the recognition of Thee as their Father and in the understanding that they are Thy children.

"We strive to abolish all that prevents the unity of Thy children being realised, so that caste, colour, race may no longer divide, that the barriers erected by man may fall and a new light and a new hope come to the world of matter.

"We seek to inspire and enthuse all those pioneers and reformers of every kind who desire to uplift their fellows, so that they may realise they are guided from on high and know that the divine blessing rests on their labours.

"To that end we pray and labour, seeking to bring Thy children closer to Thee and Thee nearer to Thy children."

Chapter Nine

'A SPARK OF THE DIVINE'

NONE would deny that one of the most celebrated, gifted writers to have lived this century was George Bernard Shaw. And what a meeting of minds it must have been when GBS agreed to be interviewed by Hannen Swaffer.

The meeting was arranged after Shaw, in "The Times," expressed gratitude for the many messages of sympathy he received after his wife's death.

Then 87, Shaw stated that he was "awaiting my own turn in perfect serenity." Shaw added: "I feel that I do not count for very much. You and I, we do the same thing. We go on telling people a lot of things. That is very nice, but nothing ever happens."

Swaffer asked Shaw what he expected to face when he, too, died. "When I die, I go," he replied. "I never did—and I do not—believe in individual survival. I do not think anybody could believe in it and realise what it means."

Hannen Swaffer's interview with Shaw caused a sensation. Subsequently it was arranged to submit to Silver Birch some questions arising out of the Shaw interview.

What, the guide was asked, awaited a man like Shaw when he passed into the spirit realms? The spirit sage replied:

"What is facing him is a new experience that will delight the mind of one whose penetrating capacity has already been revealed in many ways. Apart from the initial shock that comes with the realisation that life—individual, conscious life—does not end with death, there is afterwards a wonderful awakening of all faculties of the mind and spirit, as it realises the infinite variety of experience awaiting it.

"It rejoices when it begins to understand the amount of wisdom, knowledge, learning, truth and all the appreciation of the higher forms of artistic attainment that become open to it. The joys of a liberated mind freed from the enslavement of the physical body which begins to find itself, to become aware of itself, and to taste the supernal joys of a larger existence without any of the trammels of the flesh, this is a theme that requires the knowledge of the greatest craftsman to explain.

"For no matter in what direction the questing mind will seek, whether it be in the realms of science, philosophy, art, morality, knowledge of any kind, there awaits it not only the inspiration of all the ages, but the wisdom of all enlightened souls who are ready personally to instruct those who are able to receive the new knowledge.

"What awaits him is a joyous spiritual adventure of which he will never tire. First there will be the personal links, the reunion of old friends and those beyond, then there will be the quickening unfoldment of an alert spirit as it seeks to stimulate its growth by all the wonders of a world where there are no physical limitations . . ."

In answer to other points arising out of the Shaw-Swaffer interview came the comments:

"Truth is all-important. As truth spreads, error flees, and the mists and shadows caused by ignorance and superstition begin to fade away. All over your world there are hundreds of thousands, possibly millions, who are held in bondage by the ignorance which is a gloom in their lives.

"Throughout all the ages the power of the spirit in one form or another has touched those whom you call the pioneers, the reformers, the martyrs, the teachers, those who are the advance guard of every century, and these have held aloft the shining prize of truth.

"And because they have had some vision, because they have been touched by a power that transcends all the forces known in the material world, they have shed a lustre on their generation; they have enabled beings to pierce that veil of darkness which surrounds their lives; they have taught those who are willing how to strike off the fetters that chain them.

"They have enabled some souls to be released from their prison-house of darkness; gloom has been dissipated in some lives. As a result, gradually, very gradually, the forces of enlightenment have grown all over the world and the forces of ignorance have receded.

"Now, all over your world, man is on the march; he has tasted liberty in one form or another; liberty of the body, liberty of the mind, liberty of the spirit. All who have helped to rescue man from the forces which have chained him to prejudice, superstition or ignorance are shining lights in the long procession of man's pageant through history.

"Only in moments of tiredness and despair does the soul feel that it has failed; in moments of exaltation it realises it has come into its own and shed a ray that has helped others to climb towards the eternal light . . .

"Yes, there is a life force, of that there is no doubt. Life exists because there is a power which gives it energy, which is its dynamic. What that force is, none in your world can say. It is beyond examination by all instruments of science; it is beyond all chemical analysis; it is beyond all material investigation.

"There is death, as you see it, and there is life. We understand quite simply that spirit is life, and life is spirit. The material world is but the shadow caused by the eternal light of the spirit. The material world is the shell; the reality is the spirit.

"The spirit is that which gave life where there was unconsciousness; the spirit is that which enables you to be aware of yourself; the spirit is that breath, that divine breath, that was breathed into man, and he became a living, conscious being.

"It is the spirit, which makes man divine, which raises him from his ancestral slime; it is the spirit which distinguishes him from the beasts of the field; it is the spirit in him which enables him to render acts of service to his fellows; it is the spirit in him which makes him altruistic and unselfish; it is the spirit in him which inspires him always to reach out to the highest of which he is capable; it is the spirit within him which whispers when he will listen. You are not material, you are divine, part of the power which guides and directs the whole of the universe and all that it contains.

"In man, this cosmic spirit, this life force, is individual. Man is an individuality, a spark of the divine fire; man is an integral part of the infinite intelligence that some call God, and I, the Great Spirit of life. The grave cannot touch the spirit; the fires of cremation cannot extinguish the spirit; there is nothing in the whole wide universe that spells extinction to an infinite spirit.

"So by virtue of the natural law, the law which I did not make, the law which has always existed and always will exist, man, through the act of death, which is but the act of dissolution, discards the physical body through which he has manifested, steps out of it and begins to express himself in the final body of ether, or the spirit—call it what name you will—which has been slowly preparing itself for this consummation.

"Death does not say farewell to man as an individual; death heightens his individuality; death is one more rung in the ladder of his individual evolution; and he emerges from death as an individual, with his consciousness intact, with his memory in no way impaired, with all the faculties of mind and spirit ready to give him a larger service, because they are freed from the limitations of a physical body with its cramping, restricting, five poor senses."

Hannen Swaffer, as the leading journalist of his day, wrote

millions of words . . . and had millions of fans who read his every word. Editor of several national newspapers, he rapidly became the celebrity celebrities longed to meet. Amongst these was actress Mary Pickford, "the world's sweetheart," for whom Swaffer arranged a sitting with Silver Birch. Here, in his own unaltered words, is how he described their meeting:

The Silver Birch sitting provided fresh confirmation of what is often stressed when actors and actresses, artists or composers sit—the great importance, from the point of view of the spirit world, of any film, play, composition or work of art that spreads knowledge or inspires large numbers of people.

Here, copied from a record of the sitting, are extracts that will be of general interest.

Silver Birch: "Now, to the little lady who comes from across the water. You know you are much beloved by many who are here today and that for many years in your life you have been conscious of the love that streams towards you from those who have passed through the change which people call death. That is so, is it not?"

Mary: "Yes."

Silver Birch: "And this love and this guidance have been realities in your own life, time and time and time again, for whenever difficulties have raised their heads and you have not known where to turn, the guidance of the spirit has shown itself with indisputable clarity and you have gone forward without hesitation to perform the task in front of you. Do I speak clearly?"

Mary: "Yes."

Silver Birch: "However, you could become more conscious of the love of the many people who are bound to you by ties of affection. Did you but realise it, the whole pattern of your life is one of great guidance. You have been led step by step all the way. When, if you had known at first what was in front of you, it all would have seemed impossible of attainment, as you have put one foot forward, so the way has been cleared to enable you to put the other foot forward; and so progress has been consistent and has been maintained.

"You have been of tremendous service because you have striven to radiate that love which has been given to you.

"You may not know all this, though some of it is clear to you. But in our world, a world inhabited by all the souls who are translated here from your plane of activity, we soon learn that the only real religion is service. Service is the coin of the spirit.

"He or she who strives to serve to the utmost is in turn served by other beings who return, inspired by the attracting force. And, as you have sought through your life to bring happiness and understanding and knowledge into the lives of others, so you have attracted to yourself not only your own loved ones, but radiant beings who left the earth many long years ago, and who pour out their accumulated wisdom through your instrumentality. Do you understand all I am saying to you?"

Mary: "Yes, I think I do."

Silver Birch: "You are regarded here as an ambassador, one who sees in herself an instrument, a means of reaching large numbers of people, and you have striven to preach this simple gospel of the reality of the invisible, where all strength and power and majesty and might reside. And so it has been throughout the whole of your life that material obstacles have been removed again and again and you have been able to go forward.

"Now I want to say to you that soon you are to set the seal on your labours; the crown will be placed upon them and you will reach the pinnacle of attainment. All that your heart desires will find fruition in the days that lie before you."

Lord Northcliffe, who invariably discloses his presence at any sitting at which I am present, then gave Mary his greetings. I did not know, but when she and Fairbanks first came to London and they were mobbed everywhere by vast crowds, Northcliffe placed his Surrey home at their disposal as a retreat.

Then Fairbanks spoke of his regrets for what had happened at the end of his and Mary's marriage. I refrain from doing more than mention the fact briefly.

"I hold no bitterness against any human being, on earth or off the earth," said Mary, "only against my own wrong-doing."

"Do not magnify that," replied Silver Birch. "If the ledger of your life were to be drawn up now, the so-called wrong-doings would be very few compared with all the unselfishness and the service you have rendered. You will never know until you come here how much good you have done for so many people.

"You have brought joy to millions of people. You have enabled them to forget for a while the little sorrows, their cares and aches, their troubles and stresses, and the storms that mean so much to them. In your own way, through your own desire, you have given service, and service is all that matters.

"When everything else is forgotten and stripped away, when wealth has faded and power has dissolved, when rank and birth are forgotten, when creed lies in the dust, the character you have earned by your life of service will endure for all time. And it is that character shining through your body that I see, and I rejoice in meeting a soul who has done some good. That is what I think about your wrong-doings.

"There is nothing for you to fear. You can go straight ahead. You wish me to speak frankly?"

Mary: "Yes."

Silver Birch: "You do not want to make lots of money. What you want to do is to do the greatest for good that you can. Isn't that so?"

Mary: "Yes."

Silver Birch: "That motive brings its own reward, and the other is automatic. It is given to you for the single purpose of giving you confidence and there is nothing to fear. Have no fear in your heart. Fear disturbs vibrations. You know about vibrations?"

Mary: "Yes, I know something about them."

Silver Birch: "Fear disturbs the atmosphere. If your heart is full of unbounded, unremitting confidence, if your soul is full of indomitable resolution because your mind has knowledge of spiritual verities, that cannot fail in a world where all values are changing.

"Nothing in the world of matter can touch you, the real you, the indestructible, infinite, eternal you. You can go forward with the full knowledge that the power which is behind you, guiding you, upholding you and sustaining you, is the mightiest power in the universe, the power of love that seeks to use you as a greater instrument of service for the Great Spirit of all life, to make known His love and His wisdom, His truth and His knowledge, to those who still know nothing about these things.

"Sometimes in the silence of your chamber you have shed tears because you think, or you have thought, you have failed. You have not. The road lies straight in front of you and the glorious promise of fulfilment will be attained. I hope I have helped you."

Mary: "Thank you very much."

Silver Birch: "No. I never accept thanks. Thanks should be rendered to the Great Spirit, whose servants we all are. I strive to perform this task and I do it with willingness and cheerfulness, and if anything I have said has been of help, then it is because I am going about my Father's business. Perhaps some time we will meet again and I can be of further service to you.

"Till then, look up, not down. Remember that light and love stream in abundance from the infinite source, which possesses an infinite storehouse. Fill yourself from that rich, vast treasury. It is yours for the asking. And go on writing."

To the circle, the guide said:

"May the power of the spirit remain with you as an inspiring force and may you become increasingly conscious of the gifts with which you have been endowed and, developing them, render service to those less fortunate than yourselves, so that your lives are truly worth while the living."

Then, just before he gave up control of the medium, the guide gave Mary a final message. "Your mother says I mustn't go away until she reassures you that her love is undying," he said, "that she never forgets that which you have done for her and that she is repaying what she considers to be that debt. She would not let me go."

Mary: "But I owe her so much. Not in ten lives could I repay it."

Silver Birch: "Well, you may have more than ten lives."

Mary: "More than a cat? I shall have eighteen lives! I shall come again one day to England to live."

Silver Birch: "Oh, it's not the first time you have come here in life. But that's another story."

Mary: "Just one little thing . . . would you tell me one little thing about me—my English self?"

Silver Birch: "It goes back more than two centuries. We shall have to meet again. I am going now. I cannot hold the medium any more."

Mary, it seems, had long believed herself to be the reincarnation of a girl who lived in England over two centuries ago. I forget now her reason for accepting this as being true.

Anyway, having been born as Gladys Smith, in Toronto, she is proud of her British origin.

'The tears of mourners'

"Oh, Great White Spirit, we strive to attune ourselves and harmonise ourselves with the power which is responsible for the whole of life.

"We recognise a ruling, directing intelligence, not in any personified form, but as the supreme law which controls every facet of activity throughout the whole of the universe, no matter what aspect is studied, no matter what secret is unearthed, no matter how far into the highest heights or how deep into the lowest depths there is research or investigation.

"All that is discovered comes within the framework of Thy natural laws. We do not recognise that anything can be supernatural or miraculous, for we see a universe ruled by law and order and with Thy divine spirit brooding over all.

"Because we know that spirit is responsible for life, we desire to draw attention to that reality and to all the laws of the spirit so that, knowing their operation, there can come to the physical world a new light, a new understanding and a new hope, and all the systems of life be enriched thereby.

"So many go through their earthly pilgrimage deaf and blind to all the wondrous beauties of spiritual realities that we strive to teach which could be theirs, and of the joy which they could have.

"This knowledge could banish much sorrow and weeping; it could dry the tears of mourners, remove the ache from their hearts, the load that makes their shoulders bowed down, and give them a strength of certainty and purpose that would equip them more fully for the great adventure which their life should be.

"And so always we strive to spread knowledge wherever it can be accepted, so that those whose hearts are touched, whose minds are open and whose souls are ready may be able to take fresh heart from the knowledge that they are never alone, that the wealth of the power of the spirit is at their disposal and that supreme love covers all things wisely and well. That is the task on which we are engaged.

"This is the prayer of Thy Indian servant who seeks to serve."

Chapter Ten

'THE GREAT SPIRIT CANNOT FAIL'

SPIRITUALISM has its enemies in the Beyond as well as in this earthly world! This surprising statement was made by Silver Birch when he was asked whether there was any organisation on the Other Side directed against Spiritualism.

"Yes, it is always part of the trouble," said the guide. "It is not the organised opposition in the sense in which it is told of the war in the heavens between the fallen angels and the good angels; that is only a symbolic picture.

"There are, unfortunately, forces which are not charitably disposed towards the spread of truth, wisdom and knowledge, and wherever they can they seek to use their influence. You find them at nearly all gatherings like this; but where the gatherings are harmonious, where there is real co-operation between earthly members and those in our world, then they are powerless to penetrate.

"It is when conditions are as chaotic as they have been—they are gradually improving—when the very atmosphere is rent with discord, that these forces can best succeed, and that explains a good deal of the interference with messages that go wrong. It is a kind of sabotage, and watchfulness has to be exercised. That is why it is unwise for individuals to attempt the unfoldment of psychic faculties when they are alone. There is no power there to enable a control or guide to build up sufficient strength to ward away the interlopers and the undesirables.

"The world of spirit is entirely composed of human beings who once lived on earth. It is not a world full of angelic cherubim. It is a world filled with a variety of human beings ranging from the very poor in spirit to the highest in saintliness. It is composed of the people who have come to it from your world, and until all people in your world live lives that are clean, unselfish, filled with service and kindliness, there will always be a proportion in our world who include the undesirables and those who will still have to be helped and watched. That is the whole reason."

"But," said a regular circle member, "if you have undesirables who throw a spanner in the works, could not people like yourself deal with them?"

"We do as far as this is possible," answered the guide, "but do not forget that a lot of them are not amenable to our influence. We cannot reach them. They become amenable to our influence only when they are touched in some way so that they are ready to be helped. You must appreciate that they cannot harm us. They can try to get near earth, to which their own condition more closely approximates. The trouble arises, not in our world as such, but only when we ourselves have to lower our vibrations to come down to earthly vibrations, and when we are coming closer to the level on which they themselves exist."

"When," said the sitter who was asking these questions, "some of those living in this world make a nuisance of themselves, people go up to them and use their skill to put them right. You cannot do that."

"Your skill," was the reply, "consists in condemning them to death and sending them into our world to create another problem there."

"But with some individuals," persisted the sitter, "we can tell them where they are wrong, and probably put them on the right path."

"And probably not as well," said Silver Birch.

"We can put them in prison," said another member of the

circle, "but it does not correct their minds or stop them. It is not a remedy. How seldom it is that you can persuade people to change their minds."

"It is not always very easy in your world to trace the ones responsible for misdeeds," said Silver Birch, "and they can hide themselves behind others. But there is a great difference between your world and ours. Ours is one in which individuals can live in the sphere for which their evolution fits them. In your world, people of different attainments live on the same physical level. But it has its advantage as well.

"But do not exaggerate the extent of this interference or opposition. It is not large in comparison with the effort that is being made in the other direction, but it does exist. And, over and above all that, there are still the fanatically-minded exponents of sectarian thought who continue to exert their opposition."

"Are those the worst of them all?" was the next question.

"No," said Silver Birch, "they are not as bad in most cases because the number of those who are conscious of what is going on is very small. The large majority live in a kind of dream fantasy that is the result of their fixed and closed minds."

A letter from a Roman Catholic was read to Silver Birch at another meeting of the circle. The writer quoted the teaching of his Church against Spiritualism. But, in his perplexity, he admitted that if spirit communication was true then "it would be wonderful to the people of the world." He also said that a result of proving Survival would be "more love among people on earth, less sin and war."

"Let us rejoice," said Silver Birch, in his reply, "that one soul has seen at least a glimmer of light and is struggling, amidst difficulty, to understand the relationship of this light towards what he has believed to be the truth as he has received it. At least he is asking questions, and when that stage is reached it is the beginning. Tell him to persevere with his questions, to prove all things, hold fast to that which is proved true, and to discard all that which cannot come within the range of proof or reason.

"Tell him that he makes many statements. Is he sure that they are all true? Where he cannot prove them he should ask, 'Are they reasonable?' If his mind, which is the gift of the Great Spirit, rejects some of them afterwards as unreasonable, then let him discard them and build his religion only on that which will withstand all test, inquiry, examination, criticism, doubt and will remain firm."

The guide went on: "It would take too long to deal with each statement in turn, but as one example he says that 'God said to Moses . . .' How does he know that 'God said to Moses . . .'? Until he can prove that, or deduce reasons to show that at least it comes within the bounds of credibility, it is not sufficient to say 'God said to Moses.' Then, what follows must be subjected to the scrutiny of reason. Even if it could have been said, has it any application today?

"If he examines and inquires he will find that much which he has accepted in days gone by as being true will not stand the test of inquiry, and he will build his religion on the foundations of knowledge. And, when the winds of doubt blow, it will not be disturbed, for knowledge is a rock. Give him my love, and tell him to persevere."

A question arose from an answer given by Silver Birch in which he said that every experience, every action, word and thought played its part, however small it might be, in life. The query asked by a woman was, "How can we control our thought successfully to enable us to be sure of our words and actions?"

The answer was: "Tell her to grow in stature by seeking to discipline herself mentally and spiritually, to learn to exercise control over every aspect of being, to assert supremacy of the superior spirit which should take control and regulate all the activities of the instrument through which it manifests.

"Self-discipline through determination to assert the mastery of the spirit is the only way. There are no prescribed text books, but the simple growth of the soul, as it learns to allow its inherent strength to take charge, prevents the brain from being an undisciplined disciple of a controlled instrument."

"Is there not a danger," began the next query, "of people using Spiritualism merely to concentrate on communion with their own loved ones and thereby losing sight of their duty and dimming their vision of the Great Spirit?"

"There is always the problem that knowledge will be misused," answered the guide. "All things can be used or abused. That is one of the problems that must be faced. Of course, there are some who will see in this a means of satisfying their own misery, and it is right that where there is sadness it should be assuaged.

"It is right that grief should be lightened and sorrow driven out. Do not deprecate the means by which those who mourn are comforted. That is very necessary, and it often is the turning point in their lives. Once the ache is healed and the tears are dried up, the heaviness dissipated, and the load lightened; once knowledge has driven out ignorance, it would be sheer selfishness to persist if there were nothing in the desire except the concern over their two selves.

"Wisdom dictates that as being rational, but I think you will find—and here again I am generalising and there may be exceptions—that where such communication has been well established, the door having been opened, others will make their presence felt and seek to use the new channel as a means of enlightening others.

"My long, long experience has confirmed the wisdom of the 'judge not' exhortation. It seems so easy to criticise others. But, alas, it is so true that we can only do so when in possession of all the circumstances that would warrant fair criticism. If all people ceased to worry about the selfishness of others and had a little more thought about their own defects and how they could be improved, perhaps there could be more progress in your world."

At meetings of the Hannen Swaffer Home Circle members usually chatted quietly amongst themselves and with guests as the medium slipped quietly, peacefully and naturally into trance. Once money was mentioned during the short pre-seance discussion. This led the guide to comment:

"All that has to be achieved in your world is achieved from the spirit, the human spirit, that has determined to conquer because, whether it knows it or not, it is part of divinity and it demands expression. The strength of all pioneers comes not from anything material, but from the spirit, whether it be the ceaseless urging from within, or the inspiration from without.

"Unfortunately, your world is still in the clutches of materialism. It thinks in terms of money; it reckons as higher the one who has more wealth; it grades not according to character but according to earthly riches, position, title, birth. But none of these is enduring; they are but the outward trappings, they are not part of reality.

"The true scale of values is dependent upon the spiritual growth of the individual, and that he achieves for himself wholly and solely by his life, by his actions, by his conduct. Money cannot buy character; money cannot buy spiritual growth; money cannot promote spiritual stature. Those, every individual must attain for himself by his own exertions, and growth is not dependent upon whether you are born in a humble home or in a castle. The exercise of the spirit is for all men. There are many surprises when death comes and the earthly trappings fall away and the soul reveals itself, and knows itself for what it is, and not for what is has pretended to be.

"I do not mean that those who possess wealth are the spiritual inferiors of all those who are materially poor. No! I mean that money has nothing whatever to do with spiritual growth, that your evolution is determined by your life and by nothing else. Unfortunately, you who live in a world of matter, confronted with so many material problems, too often get a faulty perspective. But always hold on to the spiritual truths, for these will endure, and the riches of the spirit, once you have obtained them, can never be taken away from you. These are eternal possessions.

"I look forward to the time when the power of the spirit will pour into your world through millions of channels, not as it does now, through a few and in sporadic bursts, but when it is all part of a normal process of life; when the barriers between the two states of life have been broken down; when the gifts of the spirit, which all possess, are naturally trained in schools; and when the recognition of the nearness and oneness of all parts of life is clearly understood. I look forward to the time when your world knows that it is part of a vast universe, and those who live in it have their eyes opened so that they can see around and about them the denizens of the larger life who are their constant companions. What a kingdom of heaven that will be!"

"What," asked an inquirer, "is the best way of introducing the teachings of Spiritualism to strangers?"

"That is a very hard question," commented the guide. "It all depends who it is," said Hannen Swaffer.

This was Silver Birch's answer: "You must recognise that each comes with a differing need; each is at a different level of spiritual growth. Some require, very necessarily, the sound of the voice that has been stilled, the touch of the hand that has vanished, the demonstration that love continues. The one they love is all they are interested in, and quite rightly so. Others are not concerned with the personal element; they see a scientific approach, others a religious problem, others a philosophical problem, and others are not ready. There is an answer for each one.

"All that we can say is just this; here is that which is true; life goes on beyond the grave and you, the individual spirit, will persist. Come and try for yourself, by any reasonable test, that what we say is true. In the end that will bring conviction to all reasonable men and women. With the unreasonable you can do nothing."

"Is today's teaching from the spirit world comparable with the teachings of the Nazarene?" the guide was asked.

Silver Birch told those present: "I find it very hard to understand why they still believe words in ancient books, the truth of which they cannot establish, or words that flow from the lips of men, dressed in some different garb from their own, and ascribe to them authority, even though there is not one whit of evidence to show what they are saying is part of an eternal verity. And yet, when the ones they love—flesh of their flesh and spirit of their spirit—come to them still full of life, they are rejected because their return does not conform to some pattern of the past."

One of the sitters commented: "In some cases it is too personal. It is too close, and people don't want to change their lives. They know that if they did believe it they would have to change. I am not criticising, but they have not the moral courage to acknowledge the complications."

"Then," said the guide, "they are hurting themselves and the ones they love. There are some who would prefer to mourn rather than to know. All knowledge is the gift of the Great Spirit. Those who spurn knowledge harm themselves. If light is offered you and you say, 'I am content with darkness,' yours is the responsibility."

Again a sitter commented, "That is why you say that we have got to be ready for it."

"Yes," said Silver Birch. "I always see my mission as twofold. One is purely destructive and the other constructive. First, to destroy all those weeds which have choked the human soul for too long; the weeds of falsity encouraged by the churches; all the nonsensical, revolting and sometimes blasphemous doctrines offered in the name of religion. All these must be extirpated, for they prevent life being lived as it should. That is the destructive part.

"The constructive part is to offer knowledge, showing how reasonable, how simple, how beautiful and how true it is to all who are ready to receive it. The two tasks go hand in hand, and I am unconcerned with those who dislike any criticism of venerable falsehood. I have seen too many of the results in your world and in mine.

"It is not easy to work in your world, but that is where our labours are so necessary. Hold on always to the truths that bring you freedom of spirit and liberty of soul. Rejoice that your minds have been enfranchised and no longer do you live warped, thwarted and distorted lives. There are too many souls that are cramped, only because they do not allow themselves the fullness of expression which could be theirs.

"Here we are offering them keys that unlock the prison of ignorance, so that they can step out of its gloom into the light, the sunlight of spiritual truth. Liberty is always preferable to slavery; slavery is wrong and liberty is right. All who encourage slavery are obviously wrong; those who fight for liberty are obviously right."

A member of the circle made a comment which drew this reply: "Every soul has to find reality at some time. The task can be delayed, but it cannot be averted for ever."

"In other words," said the commentator, "everybody, even the most lowly, has got to become spiritually developed."

"Yes," answered Silver Birch, "through aeons of time. We are concerned with the reality of life, trying to teach your world that it cannot find peace or real happiness in shadows. Shadows exist because they are cast by the light, and the light is spiritual reality. We desire always to draw attention to the vast potentialities of an infinite spirit, not only ruling throughout the universe, but in fragment, resident in every individual.

"It is within that you will find all that vast treasury where true riches are stored. It is within that you will find the strength to help you in times when you need it and when all the resources of matter fail; when all earthly friends have fled; when you seem to be alone, uncared for and neglected. Even then, you can know that the warmth, the companionship and the love of beings from another world are still with you."

Responding to a question, Silver Birch reminded sitters: "You have to go on with your great fights. Do not be afraid of having controversy or strife in which these principles are involved. In the end you will succeed in making this knowledge accepted by the majority of mankind, not because you have submitted to what you know to be wrong, not because you have temporised, not because you have sought refuge in subterfuge, but because you have been determined to stand by the truth no matter what the cost may be.

"All those who are afraid of the consequences are weaklings. Character is not forged that way. Let those who are the instruments of the world of spirit be proud of persecution; let them welcome all the assaults from wherever they may come; and let them hold their heads proudly in the air so that all men may see by their bearing and their conduct that they are ready to be tried and tested to the end, but they will endure."

And, because it was spring, the guide, stating that the season of eternal hope contained a lesson for everyone, said: "Now, finally, I want to say this is the time of fulfilment of rejoicing, for a new life is being born into your world. The season of resurrection is upon you. On all sides you will witness the handiwork of the divine creator as new beauty will pulse through your world in millions of different forms.

"Now you are to behold the dawn of a new creation that comes regularly as part of the natural joy of life. It is accompanied by reinvigoration, by strength and by the growing rays of the sun.

"Fill yourself with this new life which spells hope, confidence, trust, founded on laws that can never fail, for always there is the demonstration given to you that life continues, no matter how long it has slept and that the power which fashioned life is eternal and that power is resident within each one of you.

"There is no cause, then, for fear or pessimism, for weariness or hopelessness. Rest yourself on that knowledge founded upon the certainty of unfailing natural law, and may the Great Spirit bless you all."

Then, at another springtime sitting, the guide uttered these words, which are as noteworthy for their majesty as their simplicity:

"You are witnessing now part of the pageantry of nature. You see nature garlanded with all the beauty of spring. The new life sings its paean of praise, its tribute to the divine composer.

"All around is evidence of the constancy of the eternal laws. The life that slept in the darkness of winter, hidden beneath the snows, has begun to make its appearance. The heralds of spring are to be seen on every hand.

"The Infinite Gardener displays His handiwork with an artistry that no mortal can imitate. Soon you will witness the crescendo of the seasons as all that which is in bud will flower, and beauty will reign in profusion in your midst.

"Summer will follow spring as autumn follows summer and winter follows autumn. The eternal cycle has always revolved, the eternal cycle will always revolve. You, too, will emerge from the winter of your life into the spring and summer as you attain the fullness of your own innate divinity.

"See in all this the sign that the Great Spirit cannot fail. If you but allow the power to flow through you, if you but make yourselves accessible, you can enjoy all the richness that comes with wisdom that is founded on the knowledge that can be yours.

"Men may disappoint you; those in whom you place your trust may fail you. You may be cheated by the laws of your country, by the regulations imposed upon you by parliaments, but the Great Spirit cannot fail because the laws of the Great Spirit are perfect.

"Only you are the impediments. Drive out the darkness of your ignorance, live in the radiant sunshine of knowledge and you will enjoy the kingdom of heaven on earth."

'The grave does not part'

"May the power of the Great White Spirit bless you all. Let us attune ourselves to the majestic power which fashioned all life and holds every facet of it within its embrace of love.

"Oh Great White Spirit, it is of thee that we desire to speak, to find the words that will strive, in clumsy fashion, to express Thy majesty, Thy divinity, Thy omnipotent law which operates throughout a universe which is boundless.

"We desire to reveal some of the rich treasury of the spirit that men and women whose hearts are filled with fears and whose minds are clouded with dismay may know how to turn to Thee, to find Thee and thus to find that assurance which will tell them all is well, divinely well.

"It is part of our purpose to strip away all the falsities, all the foolish error, all the ignorance and misapprehension that have prevented Thy children from beholding Thee as Thou art, the law, perfect in execution and in operation, the law which never fails or falters, the law which makes no mistakes.

"We see a universe in which provision has been made for every being, animate or inanimate, and for every circumstance.

"Nothing is hidden from Thee; there are no secrets or riddles. Thou knowest all, for all comes within the domain of Thy law. And so it is to this law which we point, the law which has always been in operation, the law which always will be in operation, so that Thy children may learn to harmonise their lives in co-operation with Thy laws, so that all the darkness, all the evil, all the chaos and misery may be banished and light may reign for ever in their midst.

"It is part of our task to reveal that love is deathless, that life is infinite, that the grave does not part those who are bound to one another by the indissoluble tie of love; that all obstacles can be surmounted and all barriers broken down when love calls to its own and the mightiest power in the universe streams through many instruments so that love can be united once again.

"We desire to reveal all the richness of the spirit, the divine, infinite spirit, inexhaustible in its nature, that awaits man's service when he has learnt to evolve himself and by so doing thus equip himself for the part which he is destined to play.

"This is the prayer of Thy Indian servant who seeks to serve."

Chapter Eleven

'MIND IS KING'

EVEN today—almost 2,000 years after he was born—the question of the rightful place to be accorded to Jesus occasionally occurs within Spiritualism. Some say he was a mortal man, but one with a superb array of quite natural psychic faculties which he often demonstrated. Still others aver that he is indeed the Son of God, a divine being.

Not surprisingly the subject of Jesus and other salient topics were often discussed when Silver Birch bridged the two worlds and communicated for 90 minutes or so. And how quickly the time sped by at sittings, as anyone who attended can vouch.

Interestingly it was a clergyman who wrote, asking for this point to be put to the ever-patient, ever-loving, ever-understanding spirit mentor: "Where does Silver Birch place Jesus Christ in the scheme of the universe? What is the difference, if any, between Jesus the man and Jesus the Christ?"

"The Nazarene," replied the guide, "is the last of the prophets or teachers who came to your world, in whom the fullness of the power of the spirit was made manifest in a form such as it had never been made before or since. There is no mystery about his birth. There is no mystery about his death. He was a man like other men, coming into the world of matter and leaving the world of matter in accordance with the natural laws of the Great Spirit. Never before his day and never since his day has so large a measure of inspiration been received in your world. He came to fulfil a task, to teach certain fundamental truths that had been neglected, buried beneath the debris of creed, ritual, ceremony, myth and fable. He attracted the attention of those whom he sought to teach.

"He exercised, after choosing the band of men who could help him, those gifts of the spirit with which he was endowed. He was a medium, using exactly the same gifts, spiritual gifts, that mediums are using today. He never tarnished his gifts. His gifts functioned strictly in accord with all psychical law. There were no miracles, no suspension of the natural laws, no abrogation of them and no interference with them. The demonstration of these gifts aroused the attention of the people, and then he proceeded to teach them the simple, eternal, fundamental truths of the spirit which have been stressed by all the inspired teachers throughout all the centuries in which man has trod your planet.

"The rest is known—the incurring of the wrath and displeasure of the conventional and the orthodox. But it is necessary to issue a strict warning that there has been so much tampering with the scanty record. There has been much interpolation, so that all you have is very gravely suspect. You can discount all the stories of miraculous happenings, for they did not occur.

"As to the second part of the question, the same individual, the same man—who is not the Great Spirit, not the power which created and fashioned all life and endowed mankind with part of its own divinity—is still at work, still using his gifts and his powers, which have been greatly developed, to help the humanity that he loved and whom he came to serve.

"No service is done to him by abrogating him to a position which he does not occupy, by claiming that he sits on the right hand of the Father, or that the Nazarene and the Great Spirit are identical and interchangeable terms. The Nazarene requires no worship, no servitude, no prostration in front of him, no bending the knees, but only that his life shall be an example to others and that they shall go and do greater things. This is but a very sketchy outline of a very large subject."

"What is the Christ spirit?" asked a member of the circle.

"These are merely words," answered the guide. "You have to go back to the days when it was believed that certain people were anointed to indicate that they had preference over others. Usually it was done to those of royal birth. 'The Christ' means 'the anointed one.' That is all."

"I can never understand," was one comment by a member of the circle on another occasion, "why you say Jesus was the greatest of the masters or teachers and that he lived an exemplary life."

"I have never said that the Nazarene lived a perfect life," said the guide. "All that I have said, the most I have said, was that he was the greatest expression of the power of the spirit that has ever come to your world, that through him you see the most of the Great Spirit, or the spirit power, that has ever been made manifest in any teacher; that he is the culmination of spirit power in a long line of teachers. I have never said that the Nazarene's life was perfect because that life had to be in conformity with the habits of the people with whom he dwelt."

"Do you regard his teachings as the highest?" asked another member.

"Unfortunately," said Silver Birch, "so many of them have become adulterated. I do not say that his teachings are the highest; all I say is that the essence of the teaching is there, as it was in all other cases, but never before was one man so gifted in so far as he possessed a mastery of psychic laws which has never been accomplished before in your world."

"Was Jesus the most evolved spirit that has been on earth?" asked one sitter, while another said, "Would it be true to say that the various spiritual gifts of the Nazarene in the aggregate total the greatest source of spirit power that has been shown?"

"No," the guide said, "it is not that. It is the mastery, it is the knowledge of the psychic law rather than the greatness of the teacher. What you have to try to realise is that here was an individual who was so in harmony with the power of the spirit that, despite all that has happened, despite all the interference with his teaching, all the interpolations and despite all the mischief that has been done in his name, it has spread all over the world in such a short time and has endured."

"On the other hand," was the comment of the member of the circle who was formerly a Methodist minister, "would not it be a very good thing if it had not spread all over the world?"

"The teaching of love being pre-eminent is good," replied Silver Birch. "There can be no quarrel about that; therefore the Nazarene who stressed that love was predominant, that love would prevail, was teaching the same simple truths that all teachers are trying to teach. You must differentiate between the teaching and the followers who have made many mistakes and whose very zeal has led them to acts which have re-crucified again and again the one they sought to follow.

"I see in the life of the Nazarene, not a perfect one from the point of it being the highest life lived by any individual in the physical world, rather do I see an instrument of the spirit so perfectly in tune with the power of the spirit that, never once, did he seek to use that power for his own ends; never once did he do anything that would react against the power which sent him into the world and the power which poured through him all the time. Never once did he do anything which would bring discredit on the mission which he was trying to achieve. There was no attempt ever to use this mighty power for any selfish end. He was in complete harmony with the law of the spirit.

"It is very hard to explain and yet it all had to be fitted to the time and circumstance of the age in which he lived. He could not be perfect, otherwise there would be no sense in the teaching that others could do better and greater things. Here was an individual to whom you can point and say, 'See what happens when the power of the spirit finds a full, rich expression.' It is an example of what can be done by all aspirants. And, in our world, the Nazarene is still the highest of whom we have any knowledge, and that, I suppose, is the only test we have.

"When I speak about the Nazarene I am conscious of the fact that I do not want to encourage any Nazarene-worship, in the same way as I do not want guide-worship. You are placed in your world to fulfil a task. You are all eternal pilgrims on an eternal march. Your equipment you must select with reason, common sense and intelligence to guide you. You will find part of your equipment in many books and in many lives. Therefore, you should select that which appeals to you, not because somebody else has said it is good, or wise, or sacred, or should be reverenced, but only because it is helpful to you on your journey. That is the only standard you need adopt.

"Take whatever appeals to your judgement, even if, later, you have to discard it in the light of fuller knowledge. Do not narrow yourself to any one book, to any one teacher, to any one guide. I am not the repository of infinite wisdom. I have no monopoly of the world of spirit. I am only one with many others trying to help your world. I make no claim to perfection or to infallibility. I am human just as all of you are human. I have merely trod a few steps further on the road of life, and, because these few steps have given me a little wider vista, I return to share that new horizon with you if you will accept what I have found."

An inquirer wrote to ask Silver Birch if Spiritualists should observe the last supper as the Christian Church does in commemoration of the Nazarene. He replied:

"If they find any satisfaction to their bodies, minds or spirits in holding any rite or ceremony, let them hold them.

We believe in the widest toleration for all. I have no desire to join in such ceremonies. It does not in any way help the Nazarene. It does not help me, and I know it will be of no help or value to thousands who have freed themselves from creedal chains.

"The greatest service that can be rendered to the Nazarene by those who regard him as their exemplar is to follow his example; to strive to lead the kind of life that renders the greatest service; to strive to unfold the powers they possess, which will enable them to comfort the mourner, to heal the sick, to assuage all those who are filled with doubt and perplexity, and help all those who need help.

"Life is more important than ceremony. Religion is not ritual, but service. Do not confuse the issues. You can expunge from all books called 'sacred' every printed word; you can excise all hymns from books of praise and worship; you can abstain from all ceremony and rite and ritual and be profoundly religious because you are living a life of nobility, of service, in which the spirit within you is finding its rightful expression.

"It is not to ceremony that we ask you to turn your attention. It is not to form, but to life itself. It is what you do. It is how you conduct yourself that matters. That is quite apart from the fact that this particular ceremony has antecedents that go back to antiquity, long before the days of the Nazarene."

Another time, asked a similar question on this subject, Silver Birch responded, "Service, that is the one great necessity."

He went on to explain: "My opinion is very clear. I see that religion has accumulated far too much from the past and a good deal of it has no association with religion at all.

"To me, religion is not worship; it is not prayer; it is not formalities that the minds of men have devised in council.

I am not concerned with ceremonies, because to me they are not essential. But always I say that if there be those who in sincerity find that any ceremony or ritual helps them, there is no reason for them to discard it.

"For myself, once you have grown out of childhood, you put away childish things. There is a real communion, the communion of spirit with spirit, that requires the attunement of two souls when mind reaches out across the barriers of earth to commune with a mind in another sphere of being—that is the best form of communion that there can be. The other encourages superstition. In truth it has nothing to do with the Nazarene."

Asked, "Why are there so few guides who were Christians on earth?" the spirit teacher said: "There were many who were Christians on earth, but they are not so well known, that is all. People forget that those who have become well known are the mouthpieces, that they have associated with them large numbers who willingly form part of their bands or groups to help in the work, and in those groups there are many who were Christians. Of course, it does not matter what they were."

This query was put to the guide, "As orthodox teaching has changed the lives of so many thousands of people, making them kind and tolerant, can this teaching be summarily dismissed?"

Silver Birch replied: "I am not concerned with any label. I am concerned only with the truth. It is no use saying to me that you should perpetuate falsity because it is unwise to disturb some, or because it has helped others, for it must always be remembered that on the other side of the account must be placed the numbers who have been harmed, who have been kept in ignorance, whose lives have been made miserable by threats of eternal torture and damnation.

"It is not fair to select just that part and say, 'This has done some good,' and to attempt to represent it as the whole. I am concerned in spreading what I know to be the truth about the laws of the spirit, and how they operate, so that those of you who are wise will frame your own lives according to this knowledge. Thus you will build systems of life—individual, national and international—that will endure because their foundations are those of truth.

"I do not worship the past just because it is the past and an aura of grandeur surrounds it. You are entitled to take from the past all that seems to you to be reasonable, true, helpful, stimulating and satisfying. And you are equally entitled to reject all that is immoral, unjust, unreasonable, unsatisfying and unhelpful. You have to become as little children so that you can see and welcome simple truth."

Questioned whether he could give an explanation of the marks of stigmata appearing on people, the guide replied: "The human mind possesses great potency, and the constant dwelling upon certain beliefs and circumstances can enable those happenings to be re-enacted on your physical body. Mind is stronger than matter, for matter is but a lower expression of mind. Mind has moulded matter so that mind can have a channel of expression. Mind is dominant, mind is king, mind is ruler. If you focus your mind on the story of the crucifixion and desire long enough and intensely enough for this to be reproduced on yourself, you will succeed in getting stigmata."

The next question was, "How would Silver Birch interpret the words, 'the love of the Great Spirit,' and 'to love our neighbours as ourselves'?"

"I would interpret both very simply," Silver Birch said, "by saying—live a life of service, forgetting self, try to help wherever you can to raise those who are fallen, drive out all iniquity, and by your own life prove that you are worthy of your divine heritage."

'To build temples of the spirit'

"Oh, Great Spirit, Thou Who art the infinite source of all life, Thou who hast fashioned and moulded the whole universe, given it a directive purpose and controlled every facet of its being, we who are endowed with Thy spirit seek to raise ourselves up to Thee, to establish a closer unity of purpose, to bind more closely the ties which unite us to Thee, to fill ourselves with Thy wisdom, Thy love and Thy power, so that we can all become greater instruments in Thy service and for the service of Thy children everywhere.

"We seek to restore all that peace and harmony which will give mankind the opportunity of fruitful service, that he may direct his energies towards spreading wellbeing and co-operation in every land, that the spectres of hunger and famine, of misery and sorrow, of pestilence and disease and of war may be abolished for ever and all may dwell in amity and concord, striving to unfold the gifts that Thou hast given them so that each may contribute to the greater wellbeing of the whole.

"We strive to bring to the surface Thy divine spirit, which resides latent within every child, so that in the ripeness of its expression Thou art made fully manifest in every life; accompanying it are all diversities of that power which knows no beginning and no end, which is infinite in its purpose and its expression.

"We strive to revive the gifts of the spirit in all their fullness, so that men may understand they are not created out of dust and matter, but are spirit of Thy spirit, and may live and regulate their lives accordingly.

"We strive to drive out sorrow and ignorance with love and understanding, to destroy barriers men have made so that from the larger life there may be a constant return to the world of matter of all those enfranchised, liberated souls who desire to prove that love, like life, is deathless and immortal.

"We strive to build temples of the spirit everywhere, so that guidance, inspiration, wisdom and truth may flow from higher spheres to man, to enable him to understand the purpose of his own life, the reason for his existence in a world of matter, that he may equip and fortify himself for that fuller, higher life that is his divine heritage.

"We strive to rescue all people from the thraldom and ignorance and superstition which for too long have held them in bondage, so that they may become free in spirit, mind and body, and live as the Great Spirit intended them to."